A SALISBURY

MISCELLANY

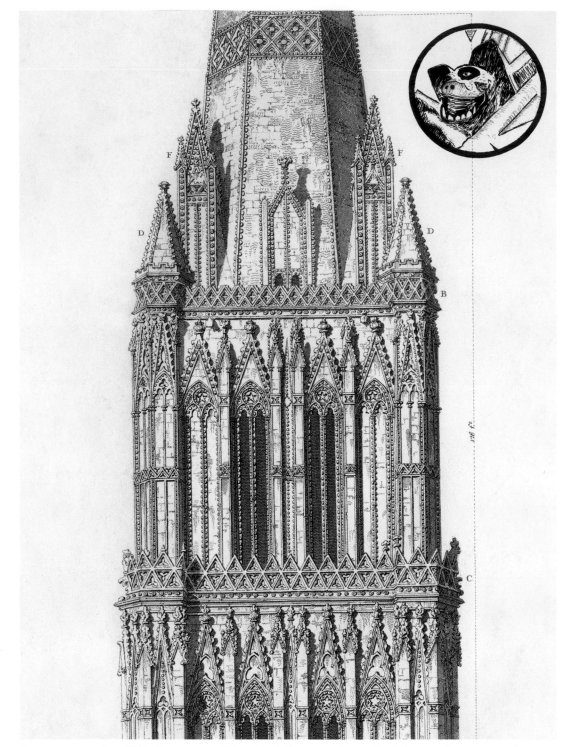

An engraving made in 1813, showing part of the cathedral tower and spire. Guided tours take visitors to the parapet where the tower and spire meet. For those who choose to look at this view from the new glass-roofed cathedral restaurant, it is worth pointing out that a row of carved wolves' heads (as in inset) can be seen along the band of decoration just below the two main pairs of lancet windows shown here (at the level marked C). Binoculars are almost essential – even the engraver has not noticed them!

A
SALISBURY
MISCELLANY

DAVID HILLIAM

SUTTON PUBLISHING

First published in the United Kingdom in 2005 by
Sutton Publishing Limited · Phoenix Mill
Thrupp · Stroud · Gloucestershire · GL5 2BU

British Library Cataloguing in Publication Data
A catalogue record for this book is available from the British Library.

ISBN 0-7509-4111-1

Bishop Richard Poore, whose vision of a new cathedral and city led to the creation of New Sarum. This statue is on the West Front of the cathedral. The building he holds has neither tower nor spire. Sadly, Bishop Poore died long before the full glory of Salisbury Cathedral was achieved.

Typeset in 10/12.5pt Latin725.
Typesetting and origination by
Sutton Publishing Limited.
Printed and bound in England by
J.H. Haynes & Co. Ltd, Sparkford.

CONTENTS

INTRODUCTION

This collection of lists is partly a guide to the cathedral and city of Salisbury, partly a history of Old and New Sarum, and partly a ragbag of oddities that hopefully will intrigue many visitors who come to enjoy this fascinating city. There are many excellent books on Salisbury – arguably no one needs another. However, it is hoped that *A Salisbury Miscellany* will provide visitors with a great deal of information in an easily digested manner.

Mixed in with facts are legends and stories to bring out the essential spirit of Salisbury – which in the past had its fair share of witches, rogues, executions and brutal excitement, but which is now a unique, vibrant modern city possessing a cathedral and a Close of matchless beauty.

Part One consists of a time chart from 'time immemorial' to the twenty-first century; Part Two is about the cathedral and the Close – including vital statistics of the cathedral itself, a list of all the statues on the West Front, a list of the famous carvings around the Chapter House and a brief description of the most important houses in the Close.

Part Three is about the city of Salisbury, its buildings, pubs, ghosts, churches and items of special interest. Also in this section are accounts of people who have made this city so memorable: bishops, royalty, writers, saints and sinners.

Finally, a short Part Four is written specially for twenty-first-century sightseers, who can visit websites before visiting actual places. An hour on the Internet will be time well spent, for there are so many websites – many of them updated daily – to whet the curiosity of those who come to enjoy this unique city, with its incomparably lovely cathedral – declared by many to be the finest view in Britain.

Salisbury Cathedral from the air. The clear geometrical symmetry of the cathedral is seen in this aerial view.

PART ONE

A Salisbury Time Chart

SALISBURY BEFORE 1066

The beginnings of Salisbury are lost in the proverbial 'mists of time'. In prehistoric times an iron age Celtic population lived in and around the area we now call Old Sarum – a hill fort about a mile and a half from the centre of the present city. The Romans called it *Sorviodunum*, which was probably a rough version of its Celtic name, and archaeological evidence shows that they began to settle in the valley below the hill fort, in Stratford-sub-Castle, on the outskirts of modern Salisbury.

Old Sarum itself was a meeting place of several important roads. However, it was not a major Roman settlement, and when the legions left Britain in about AD 410, Old Sarum again became merely an obscure and undeveloped hill fort.

The first mention in medieval history is a brief remark in *The Anglo-Saxon Chronicle*, noting that Old Sarum was the scene, in 552, of an early battle between the occupying ancient Britons and the marauding Saxons, led by Cynric, son of Cerdic, the first King of Wessex. According to tradition these Saxon leaders were descendants of the god Woden, whose name of course is forever remembered every week in the name 'Wednesday'. This battle between Woden's descendants and the luckless Celts is Salisbury's starting-point.

552	The *Anglo-Saxon Chronicle* reports that 'In this year Cynric fought against the Britons at the place called Searoburh, and put the Britons to flight.' This battle probably took place at or near Old Sarum. After this defeat, the site seems to have been abandoned.
871–99	Alfred the Great strengthens the fortifications of Old Sarum as a safeguard against the Danish invaders.
960	The Saxon king Edgar the Peaceful (959–75) holds his court at Old Sarum.
1003	Old Sarum has a narrow escape from the Danish invader, Sweyn Forkbeard, the father of King Canute. Sweyn had already destroyed Exeter and had burned Wilton, but when he sees how strongly Old Sarum is fortified, he decides to leave well alone, and returns to his ships on the south coast.
c.1004	The Saxon king Ethelred the Unready sets up a royal mint at Old Sarum. This continues to operate and is still making silver pennies in the reign of Henry II (1154–89).
1058	Two former Saxon dioceses, Sherborne and Ramsbury, are joined together to form one new diocese with the bishop's throne at Sherborne. Herman is its first bishop.
1066	William the Conqueror's victory at Hastings results in important changes throughout England. Crucial for Salisbury is William's decision, in 1075, to move the newly formed diocese of Sherborne to the hill-top fortification of Old Sarum. For the first 145 years of its existence, Salisbury grows steadily on this site.

Above: The ancient hill fort of Old Sarum as seen from New Sarum.

Below: Site of the first cathedral (1092–1220) at Old Sarum.

OLD SARUM, 1066–1220

William the Conqueror and the Norman invaders of 1066 quickly strengthened the defences of Old Sarum and began constructing a formidable castle where King William and his royal successors were often in residence. It was at Old Sarum in 1086 that William paid off his army at a great ceremonial meeting, known as 'The Oath of Salisbury'. However, Old Sarum's decline began in 1220, when it was decided to build a new cathedral (the present one) in the valley below. The main dates in the history of Old Sarum between the Conquest and the foundation of the new cathedral are:

1075   Bishop Herman of Sherborne moves to Old Sarum, where he supervises the building of the first cathedral. His new diocese comprises much of Wiltshire, Dorset, Berkshire and Hampshire. Herman becomes Salisbury's first Bishop.

1086   William the Conqueror gathers all his principal nobles to Old Sarum and demands that they swear an oath of loyalty to him. This is known as 'The Oath of Salisbury'.

1092   Bishop Osmund, Salisbury's second bishop, consecrates Old Sarum's cathedral.
        Five days later it is struck by lightning and the eastern end is badly damaged.

1099   Death of Bishop Osmund. Immediately after his death he is popularly regarded as a saint because of the miracles happening near his tomb. Three and a half centuries later, in 1457, he is officially canonised and becomes Salisbury's patron saint.

1102   Bishop Roger becomes Salisbury's third bishop. He sets about redesigning and enlarging the cathedral.

An artist's impression of the cathedral at Old Sarum, drawn by Alan Sorrell.

1189	Hubert Walter is consecrated as Salisbury's fifth bishop. Later, he becomes Archbishop of Canterbury and virtual ruler of England while King Richard I ('The Lionheart') is fighting in the Holy Land during the Third Crusade.
1194	Herbert Poore is consecrated as Salisbury's sixth bishop.
1215	King John puts his seal to Magna Carta at Runnymede, near Windsor. One of the four remaining copies of this great charter is still held in the cathedral's Chapter House. Present at the signing is William Longespée, half-brother of King John. Five years later, Longespée is to lay a foundation stone of the present cathedral (see page 62).
1217	Bishop Richard Poore, Salisbury's seventh bishop and brother of Bishop Herbert Poore, gains permission to transfer the site of the cathedral from the hill-top fortress of Old Sarum to his own land at Myrfield (Maer-felde, or 'boundary field'), in the meadows near the River Avon.
1220	On 28 April the foundation stones of the present cathedral are laid. A new Salisbury – NEW SARUM – was born.

Above: Bishop Roger, Salisbury's third bishop, 1102–39. This memorial was originally in the Old Sarum Cathedral, but was brought to the present cathedral in 1226, when the bodies of Osmund, Jocelyn and Roger were reinterred here.

Left: The well at Old Sarum – the only source of water for the entire community of clerics and military.

SIX REASONS WHY OLD SARUM
WAS ABANDONED

In 1075, just nine years after the battle of Hastings, the foundations of Old Sarum's cathedral were laid. However, conditions were difficult for the churchmen who settled there. Here are six reasons why they decided to establish a brand-new city in the meadows to the south.

1. *Old Sarum was far too small.* Situated on top of an ancient hill fort, the settlement had no space for expansion.

2. *It was too windy.* Those who worshipped in the old cathedral complained that they could could hardly hear what was being said because of the howling winds.

3. *Water was desperately scarce.* True there was a well, but no township could survive with such a pitiful water supply. Washing, drinking and meal preparations must have been a constant nightmare. Lavatory facilities must have been appalling.

4. *There was friction between churchmen and the military.* Basically, Old Sarum was a fortified camp linked to a tiny cathedral city. Soldiers and clergy were uneasy neighbours. There were constant tussles, and the soldiers humiliated the clergy by making them pay exorbitant prices for their share of the water supply.

5. *Then came the final last straw.* In 1217 an incident occurred that triggered the bishop's decision to leave the hill fort for ever and start a new city with a new cathedral.

   At Rogationtide in that year the bishop and clergy had left Old Sarum to go in procession to the nearby village of Milford. Traditionally, the Rogationtide processions involved 'beating the bounds' of the parish, and the churchmen would be wearing their holy vestments.

   When they got back, they found that the soldiers had barricaded the entrance to Old Sarum and they were forced to spend the night locked out of the city, with the soldiers jeering at them from the castle walls. This was intensely frustrating and offensive.

   Without more ado, Bishop Herbert Poore wrote to Pope Honorius II to beg permission to move to a more convenient site.

6. *The Virgin Mary appeared to Bishop Richard Poore in a dream.* According to legend, the Virgin Mary miraculously appeared to Bishop Herbert's brother and successor, Richard Poore. In a dream she instructed him to build at Myrfield – his own meadow land where two rivers flow into the Avon. Here there would be space and, importantly, a generous supply of water.

THE NEW CITY OF SALISBURY, 1220–TODAY

1220   On 28 April the foundation stones of the new cathedral are laid. The first stone is laid by Bishop Richard Poore on behalf of the Pope, the Archbishop of Canterbury and himself. Then William Longespée, Earl of Salisbury and uncle of King Henry III, lays the next stone, followed by his wife, the Lady Ela, and other noblemen and clergy. The design and construction of the new cathedral are attributed to two men: Elias of Dereham, a canon of the cathedral, and Nicholas of Ely, a master mason.

1221   'Leadenhall' (70 The Close) is begun as a dwelling for Elias of Dereham, canon of the cathedral and its architectural designer.

1225   On the Eve of Michaelmas Day (30 September), the Trinity Chapel is consecrated for worship. This is the first part of the cathedral to be finished and put into use. The Trinity Chapel is at the furthest eastern end of the cathedral, where the modern *Prisoners of Conscience* window is to be seen.

1226   The bodies of three former bishops (Roger, Osmund and Jocelyn de Bohun) are brought down from the old cathedral to be reburied in the new cathedral.

1227   The city of Salisbury is given its first royal charter, allowing a weekly market on Tuesdays and an annual ten-day fair in August.

1240–70   The cloisters – the largest in England – are constructed.

1244   Bishop Bingham builds a new bridge, the Aylswade Bridge, providing a route into the city from the village of Harnham.

1245   A chapel is dedicated to St Thomas Becket in the city's huge marketplace, and becomes Salisbury's first new parish church – St Thomas's.

1258   On 30 September, the new cathedral is consecrated in the presence of King Henry III and Queen Eleanor. The Archbishop of Canterbury officiates together with the Bishop of Salisbury, Giles de Bridport. So, after only thirty-eight years, the main body of the cathedral has now been completed. The spire, however, has yet to be built.

1261   Bishop Giles de Bridport founds the College of St Nicholas de Vaux, just south of the cathedral Close.

c.1265   The West Front is completed. Also, a separate bell tower is built (pulled down in 1790).

1266   It is recorded that on 25 March – Maundy Thursday – the cathedral is finally completed. The total cost has been £28,000.

1269   Bishop de la Wyle founds the parish church of St Edmund in the city of Salisbury. Edmund Rich had been Treasurer of Salisbury Cathedral 1222–34 during its construction, and had later become Archbishop of Canterbury. He was canonised in 1247 and his name is perpetuated by St Edmund Hall at Oxford, founded in his memory.

1307	Edward I holds a great tournament near Old Sarum. The field in which it took place is one of England's five licensed tournament fields. Tournament Road, in upper Bemerton, reminds us of this chivalric history of Salisbury.

1315	The city of Salisbury is granted permission to hold a second market day each week — on Saturdays. In the twenty-first century Salisbury still enjoys Tuesday and Saturday markets.

1331	Edward III allows the Close wall to be built, using material from the former cathedral at Old Sarum.

c.1334	Work begins on the 404ft spire. Its weight will eventually reach an astonishing 6,400 tons, bearing down on four main pillars, each 6ft in diameter. (Recent research, however, suggests that the spire was begun in the 1280s and completed by 1329. This question is still under debate.)

1346–53	Salisbury is badly affected by the Black Death. Between a third and a half of its citizens die as a result of this nationwide plague.

1377	The population of Salisbury is estimated to be about 4,800.

This extraordinary windlass, worked by manpower, dates from the thirteenth century and has been used throughout succeeding centuries to haul large items of stone and timber into the cathedral tower. It is to be seen at the level where tower and spire meet.

1384	A dramatic meeting of Parliament is held in Salisbury. At this, the Earl of Arundel publicly accused King Richard II of bad government. The King leapt to his feet and shouted: 'If you impute bad government to me, you lie in your throat! Go to the Devil!' John of Gaunt, the King's uncle, had to calm things down.

c.1400	It is estimated that at this time about a third of Salisbury's workforce is engaged in the wool trade – weavers, fullers or dyers. It is now the city's most important industry and Salisbury is the foremost cloth-making centre in England. A striped cloth known as 'Salisbury ray' is sold throughout the country and also extensively on the Continent.

c.1450	The 'strainer arches' are built to strengthen the central crossing of the cathedral nave and transepts. These are built in the perpendicular style.

1457	Osmund, the second bishop of Old Sarum, is canonised at last, 358 years after his death. St Osmund is regarded as the patron saint of Salisbury.

1523	The city of Salisbury is now the seventh largest city in England with a population of about 8,000.

1556	Three protestant martyrs are burnt to death in Salisbury in the reign of 'Bloody Mary'.
1604	Severe outbreak of the plague. About 17 per cent of Salisbury's population die.
1611	The puritanical Mayor of Salisbury tells the Tailors' Guild that their giant (now preserved in Salisbury Museum (see pages 102–3)) is 'abomynable before God and hell gapes for such ydle and prophane fellowes as delight in it'.
1612	The city of Salisbury is given a charter by King James I, releasing it for the first time from the authority of the bishop. Salisbury gains its independence at last.
1625	King Charles I visits Salisbury and borrows £1,000 from the city.
1626	Yet another outbreak of the plague. The Mayor, John Ivie, heroically struggles to cope with the problems, maintaining law and order and distributing food. His name is remembered today in the name of Ivy Street.
1644	Oliver Cromwell's troops plunder the cathedral.
1662	Salisbury is now estimated to be the fifteenth largest city in England. Clay pipes, joinery and cutlery are flourishing trades.
1665	King Charles II and his court come to Salisbury to escape London's Great Plague. Nell Gwynne, accompanying him, buys a pair of Salisbury-made scissors for one hundred guineas (£105).
1682	The College of Matrons in the Close is built by Bishop Seth Ward, a founder member of the Royal Society and close friend of Sir Christopher Wren.

The arms of Charles II on the College of Matrons.

1700	About this time it is estimated that more than a thousand lace-makers, mostly poor women and children, are making their wares in Salisbury.
1701	Mompesson House is completed, overlooking Choristers' Green in the Close. This beautiful building is now owned by the National Trust (see page 30).
1702	Trinity Hospital, a medieval almshouse, founded about 1379 in St Ann Street, is rebuilt and acquires the classical courtyard we see today.
1715	Salisbury now has its own newspaper, *The Salisbury Postman*, one of the first newspapers to be published in a provincial town.
1716	The Wren Hall is built to house the Choristers' School (56 The Close).
1729	The *Salisbury Journal* is established by William Collins, a city printer, as a successor to the *Salisbury Postman*. It costs two pence and is published on Tuesdays, one of the city's two market days. This local newspaper is still going strong in the twenty-first century.
1741	The cathedral tower is struck by lightning. Luckily the fire is soon extinguished.
1751	James Harris, who lives in Malmesbury House – next to St Ann's Gate into the Close – organises an annual Salisbury Music Festival at which the music of his friend Handel is played. Handel himself is believed to have played in the room above St Ann's Gate.
1763	Six stagecoaches now run regularly between London and Salisbury.
1766	Oliver Goldsmith's *The Vicar of Wakefield* is first printed in Salisbury, by Benjamin Collins.
1771	Salisbury infirmary, a purpose-built hospital in Fisherton Street, is opened.

SALISBURY INFIRMARY

Salisbury Infirmary, 'supported by voluntary contributions', served the city and surrounding area for over 200 years, until a new hospital opened at Odstock in 1993. Its original regulations warned that it would accept: 'No woman big with child, no child under 7 years . . . none disordered in their senses, suspected to have small-pox, itch, ulcers in the legs, cancers, consumptions, dropsies, epileptics . . .'. It seems that the doctors were determined not to have really sick people on their hands!

1780	The old Elizabethan council house in the marketplace is severely damaged by fire. The Earl of Radnor donates the present classical Guildhall (built 1787–95).

1788–91   James Wyatt is employed by Bishop Shute Barrington to 'improve' the cathedral. As a result, much of the original medieval interior is destroyed or rearranged (see pages 23–4).

1790   Destruction by James Wyatt of the old bell tower in the Close (see page 23).

An eighteenth-century engraving of Salisbury Cathedral and the bell tower that was destroyed by James Wyatt in 1790.

1795   Fifty-two stagecoaches now run regularly between London and Salisbury. This number increases to fifty-nine in 1839, carrying more than 50,000 passengers per year.

1800   The population of Salisbury is now about 7,600.

1820   The old coaching inn, the White Hart in St John Street, acquires its present classical façade.

1837   Cedars of Lebanon are planted in the lawn within the cloisters to commemorate the accession of Queen Victoria. These are still there, beautifully mature trees.

1840   The population of Salisbury is now about 10,000.

1841	A training college for schoolmistresses is established in the King's House in the Close (now the Salisbury and South Wiltshire Museum). Thomas Hardy's sisters are students here, as was the fictional Sue Bridehead, in his *Jude the Obscure*.
1847	Salisbury welcomes the first railway train 'direct from London'. The journey takes four hours; tickets cost 24 shillings 1st class, or 18s 6d 2nd class.
1847–8	St Osmund's church is built in Exeter Street, to the design of Augustus Pugin.
1849	Salisbury suffers a terrible cholera epidemic, 192 people die – one in every 45 of its inhabitants. Clearly this epidemic is caused by the appalling state of the 'canals' – which were, in effect, open sewers.
1851	The Great Exhibition is held in London and the *Salisbury and Wiltshire Journal* reports that 'A very superior case of cutlery, of Salisbury manufacture, was sent up to the Great Exhibition on Wednesday last by Mr Beach of this city.'
	Meanwhile, in this year, inquiries are held under the new Public Health Act into the unsatisfactory sanitary conditions of the city.
	Also in this year Anthony Trollope visits Salisbury and gains inspiration for Hiram's Hospital in *The Warden* as he contemplates the Hospital of St Nicholas, an almshouse near the cathedral.
1852	Salisbury follows London's example and holds the first provincial 'Great Exhibition'; 7,000 visitors come to admire the display of Salisbury's arts, trade and industry. Also in this year the Poultry Cross is given a new roof (see pages 78–9).
1859	A new covered market house is built near the marketplace, with its own connection with the newly opened railway. Nowadays this building houses Salisbury Library and Galleries.
1870	The population of Salisbury is now about 13,000.
1874	The increase in the number of tourists visiting the city by railway leads to the building of the County Hotel, near Fisherton Bridge.
1875	The last of the old canals, known as the Town Ditch, is filled in. Today it is one of Salisbury's main streets, known as New Canal.
1890	The Clock Tower in Fisherton Street is built, using part of the old Fisherton Gaol as its base.
1900	The population of Salisbury is now about 17,000.
1906	A serious railway disaster takes place at Salisbury railway station. The victims have a memorial on the north wall of the nave in the cathedral.
1914–18	Nearly 3,000 wounded soldiers are nursed in Salisbury Infirmary during the First World War. A total of 459 men and women from Salisbury lose their lives during this war.

1930	Foundation of the 'Friends of the Cathedral'. One of the first tasks to be undertaken is the rebuilding of the organ. Members are asked to subscribe 'not less than two shillings and sixpence a year'.
1935	The cathedral spire is floodlit for the first time, as part of the Silver Jubilee celebrations of King George V and Queen Mary.
1939–45	The streets of the city are filled with soldiers and airmen billeted on Salisbury Plain. Schools are filled with children evacuated from Portsmouth and other towns. Army tanks roar along the roads and children have to pull their bikes onto the pavements to make room for them. Barrage balloons float over the city to deter enemy aircraft. Luckily, Salisbury escapes the 'blitz', and the cathedral remains intact. Some bombs fall, however, and in 1941 the Dean and Chapter offer the Chapter House as shelter for people bombed out of their homes.
1949–51	The top 23ft (7m) of the spire are removed and rebuilt.
1952	A Salisbury Centenary Exhibition is held, to commemorate the exhibition held in 1852, following the London Great Exhibition.
1974	Queen Elizabeth II comes to the cathedral for the Royal Maundy Service.
1980	Yehudi Menuhin unveils the *Prisoners of Conscience* window at the east end of the cathedral. This has been designed and made by M. Gabriel Loire of Chartres.
1981	Elisabeth Frink's statue *Walking Madonna* is placed in the Close near the path leading to High Street gate.
1985	Charles, Prince of Wales, accepts the Presidency of the Spire Appeal, launched for the urgent restoration of the spire, tower and West Front of the cathedral.
1992	The population of Salisbury is now about 40,000.
2000	A great concert is held in the Close in the presence of Prince Charles to celebrate the success of the Spire Appeal. Coloured laser patterns on the West Front are part of this televised entertainment. However, the work of repair and restoration must still continue.
2004	A statue of George Herbert, sculpted by Jason Battle and donated by the Friends of Salisbury Cathedral, is installed on the West Front (see page 53).

The city, with its restored cathedral, thirty-three places of worship, 123 pubs and over four million day visitors a year, is well prepared for the century to come.

PART TWO

Salisbury Cathedral and Close

EIGHTEEN VITAL STATISTICS

A six-year-old child, seeing Salisbury Cathedral for the first time, exclaimed: 'They must have needed a lot of stuff to make that building!' He was right. The body of the cathedral is built with 60,000 tons of creamy-grey Chilmark stone, generously donated by the quarry's thirteenth-century owner. Contrasting with this colour, are the almost countless number of near-black pillars made from Purbeck marble.

1.   The height of the spire is 404ft (123m) – the highest spire in England. The spire itself, as distinct from the tower, is 180ft.

Modern carving in the cathedral workshop yard, before being installed into the fabric of the tower.

2.   Its external length is 473ft (145m).

3.   Its width is 229ft (70m).

4.   The length of the nave is 229ft (70m).

5.   The height of the interior is 81ft (25m).

6.   The sides of the cloisters are each 181ft long (56m) – the largest cloisters in England.

7.   The Chapter House is 58ft wide (18m).

8.   60,000 tons of Chilmark stone were used in the cathedral's construction.

9.   10,000 tons of Purbeck marble were needed for the pillars.

10.   2,800 tons of oak were needed to support the roof and the interior of the spire. King Henry III (1216–72) donated some of this from his royal estate at nearby Clarendon.

11.   420 tons of lead cover the roof. All this had to be transported from the Mendips, Wales or Derbyshire.

12.   About 3 acres of glass were needed to fill the windows.

13.   The weight of the tower and spire is estimated to be 6,400 tons.

14.   The cathedral was built between 1220 and 1258 – just thirty-eight years.

15.   The West Front was completed by 1265.

16.   The Chapter House was completed by 1286.

17.   The tower and spire were added between 1334 and 1365.

18.   The spire leans 27½in (69.85cm) to the south and 17½in (44.44cm) to the west.

EIGHT FACTS ABOUT THE SPIRE

No one can think of Salisbury without remembering its world-famous spire. Here are some lesser-known facts about it.

1. It is 404ft high (123m). This makes it the tallest spire in England, but the spire of the cathedral in Ulm, Germany, is higher, at 529ft (161m).

2. It has eight sides, with a trapdoor near the top, on the north-east, for the use of anyone who needs to inspect the cross or the lights. The Clerk of Works regularly makes this somewhat alarming ascent from the trapdoor to the summit.

3. The tower and spire were designed and built between 1334 and 1363 by Richard of Farleigh, who incorporated concealed metal reinforcements within his work – a daringly new innovation for that time.

4. It was struck by lightning in 1559, the year after Queen Elizabeth I came to the throne, and a split occurred in the masonry 60ft from the top.

5. A new copper vane was added in 1762.

6. Research carried out in 2004 on the wooden struts inside the spire suggest that these timbers date from between 1344 and 1376. This would mean that they were added *after* the spire had been built – probably after the hurricane that hit the cathedral in 1362.

7. The top 23ft (7m) of the spire were removed and replaced in 1949–51.

8. When Sir Christopher Wren examined the spire in the seventeenth century, he found that it tilted 27½in to the south and 17½in to the west. There is a mark on the floor of the nave, in the middle of the crossing, which indicates just how far the spire is leaning out of true.

Those with stamina and a head for heights can enjoy a spectacular visit up the tower. This involves a walk inside the triforium, followed by many steps upwards within the tower. There are breathtaking views from the external balcony, where tower and spire meet.

On several occasions over the centuries, first recorded in 1736, the spire has attracted huge swarms of gnats or flying ants – in such numbers that people have feared that the spire was on fire. In June 1952, firemen climbed to the top of the spire to deal with a threatened disaster, only to discover that the 'smoke' was a swarm of flying ants!

The timber strutting inside the spire, as seen from the floor at the top of the tower.

NINE GRUESOME RELICS

An interesting discovery was made in 1762 when the capstone at the top of the spire was being repaired. Workmen found a wooden box hidden at the very top. Inside this was a round leaden casket 5½in in diameter and just over 2in deep, containing a small piece of woven fabric.

This cloth was thought to be a relic of the Virgin Mary, to whom the cathedral is dedicated. It was probably deposited at the top of the spire to guard it against lightning or strong winds.

Other curious relics held in the cathedral during the Middle Ages included:

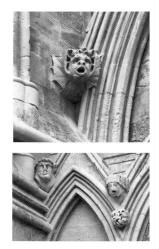

1. An arm of St Thomas Becket in a casket.

2. The chain wherwyth St Catharine bound the Devil.

3. Part of our Saviour's cross.

4. Some of the precious hair of Seynt Peter.

5. A tooth of St Macarius.

6. The jaw bone of St Stephen.

7. A finger of St Agnes.

8. A toe of St Mary Magdalene.

9. A toe of St Anne.

This list comes from *A Register and Inventory of the Jewels and Riches belonging to the Cathedral Church of Sarum*, drawn up in 1536.

The heads on this page are from the West Front of the cathedral.

ST OSMUND ACQUIRES A SAINTLY ARM

The acquisition of saints' relics was one of the stranger aspects of the medieval church. When Bishop Osmund officiated at the translation of St Aldhelm's relics in Malmesbury in 1078, he took away with him one of St Aldhelm's arms, which he donated to the cathedral at Old Sarum. What ultimately happened to this bony relic is not known. (St Aldhelm (639–70) was a Saxon saint and the first bishop of Sherborne – so he should be regarded as the first bishop of the diocese that later became the see of Salisbury.)

THREE LOCKED GATES

The Close wall – that is, the wall surrounding the large area round the cathedral – was built in 1331, using stone taken from the old Norman cathedral at Old Sarum. King Edward III gave special permission for the use of the old cathedral stone to make this wall.

Today we can still see the remains of carved heads sticking out of the wall, but sadly these have been corroded by modern exhaust fumes, and they are no longer as sharply defined as they were even within living memory. Nevertheless, there are many Norman decorative carvings to be seen here as you walk along this beautiful medieval wall.

Only three public entrance gates were made, although there is another private gate that was made specially for the Bishop – called, inevitably, 'Bishopsgate'.

1. *St Ann's Gate*, shown below, in Exeter Street. Noteworthy is the fact that Handel gave his his first concert in England in the room above the gate – that is, where the pointed medieval window is to be seen.

Notice on High Street Gate.

2. *High Street Gate*, or *North Gate*, leading directly from the High Street. The small carved figure of a king to be seen high up at the top of the gate on the cathedral side is that of King Edward VII.

3. *Harnham Gate*, or *South Gate*, at the southern side of the Close. To reach this gate, which is somewhat tucked away from view, follow the line of the path in front of the West Front of the cathedral in a southerly direction and it is only about a couple of minutes' walk away. Harnham Gate is far less 'architectural' than the other two, and has a pleasant, domestic feel about it.

The Close is firmly closed at night. All three gates are locked and anyone needing to get in or out must ask for the doors to be specially opened.

St Ann's Gate.

8,760 MARBLE PILLARS?

There is an old tradition about the cathedral – often expressed in rhyme. One version in memorable doggerel rhyme runs:

> As many Days as in One Year there be,
> So many Windows in One Church we see;
> As many Marble Pillars there appear,
> As there are Hours throughout the fleeting Year;
> As many Gates [doors] as Moons One Year do view:
> Strange Tale to tell, yet not more strange than true!

In other words, there are 365 windows, 8,760 marble pillars and 12 doors or gates.

The Purbeck marble pillars come from layers of 'dirt-beds' found in the limestone quarries in the Isle of Purbeck in Dorset. This 'marble' consists of fresh-water shellfish.

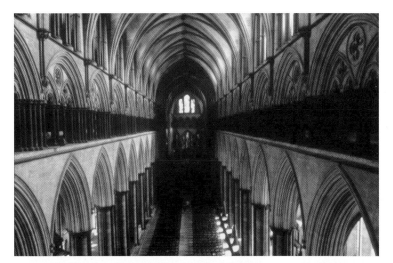

Left: Nave as seen from the walkway on the West Front, linking the north and south triforiums. This is the best place to appreciate the vast number of marble pillars.

Below, left: Walkway inside the north triforium, showing a glimpse of the clusters of marble pillars.

Below: A view of the interior of the nave roof.

FIVE DAREDEVILS CLIMBING THE SPIRE

The challenge of climbing the spire used to be a regular local sport. It was favourite entertainment during the city's annual Whitsun Fair, but the tradition died out at the beginning of the nineteenth century. On one of these occasions Arnold, a watch-maker, is reported to have wound up his watch while leaning against the weathervane. But this was tame entertainment compared with other daring feats.

1. *Old Halley's Feast.* In 1655, during the Commonwealth, when festivities of any sort were frowned upon, an old plumber called Halley was determined to enjoy himself and defy the authorities. He climbed the spire with kitchen utensils, roasted a leg of mutton and two chickens and gave himself a banquet on the top of the spire, much to the delight of the onlookers below.

2. *A surprising reward for a spire-climber.* When Charles II visited Salisbury in 1665, a man climbed to the tope of the spire and sang loyal songs to the monarch below. When he got down to the ground again, he hoped for a fat reward for his daring. However, he reckoned without the King's quirky sense of humour, for instead of receiving a bag of money, all he got were letters patent from Charles, giving him and his heirs the exclusive right of climbing all the steeples in England without let or hindrance.

3. *A kingly reprimand.* A local boy climbed the spire when George III came to the city. He sat on the cross at the top, singing and waving flags. Finally, he stood on his head on the capstone. To his disappointment, when he got down again, the King gave him a sound ticking-off for endangering his own life and setting a bad example to the rest of his subjects.

4. *A sailor's death knell.* A nineteenth-century sailor managed to climb to the top, but just as he did so the cathedral bell rang out. The shock of this sudden loud noise unnerved him. He lost his grip, fell to the ground and was killed.

5. *A souvenir for £2.* Also in the nineteenth century a Salisbury tradesman climbed to the top of the spire, fulfilling a lifetime's ambition, but he nearly lost his life when the weather vane suddenly swung round. Luckily he managed to hold on. When he reached the ground again, an American offered him £2 for his torn trousers.

Initials are to be found carved near the top of the spire – 'GE ROCHE 1578', 'FWC 1696' and others with later dates – proofs of old-time feats of daredevilry.

SIX FACTS ABOUT MAGNA CARTA

One of Salisbury Cathedral's most valuable possessions is an original copy of Magna Carta, now on view in the Chapter House.

This document is a milestone in the history of democracy, boldly asserting the fundamental supremacy of the rule of law over the power of dictatorial kings. It is a precursor to the great American Declaration of Independence, 561 years later.

Magna Carta is one of the most famous medieval documents in Europe, written just five years before Salisbury Cathedral was founded. Here are some basic facts.

1. King John (1199–1216) and his rebellious barons met 'in the meadow which is called Runnymede' – about three miles south-east of Windsor, on 15 June 1215. It was at this meeting that John affixed his seal to this charter of liberties.

2. Thirteen original copies of Magna Carta were made.

3. Only four copies now remain: one in Salisbury Cathedral; one in Lincoln Cathedral; and two in the British Library in London – one of which is illegible owing to fire damage.

4. The Salisbury copy is written on just one piece of vellum 14in x 7¼in (35.5cm x 18.5cm). Vellum is parchment made from the skin of calves or lambs.

5. John did not sign it. He put his seal to it.

6. It is written in Latin, with the letters and words placed very close together and with many traditional medieval abbreviations so as to save space. Because of this, the translation seems to be much longer than the original text.

William Longespée, half-brother of King John and of King Richard I ('Lionheart'), was present at this sealing of Magna Carta. Five years later, in 1220, Longespée laid one of the foundation stones of Salisbury Cathedral, and in 1226 he became the first person to be buried in the Cathedral (see pages 6 and 62).

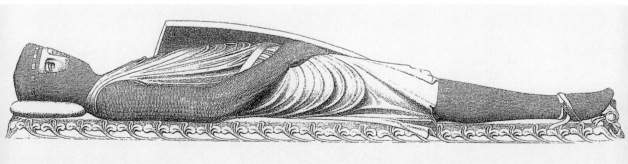

Memorial of William Longespée on the south side of the nave. (See also the story on page 62.)

NINE COMPLIMENTS PAID TO
SALISBURY CATHEDRAL

1.   '...the completest Gothic work in Europe.'

(John Evelyn (1620–1706))

2.   '... most admirable, as big I think and handsomer than Westminster, and a most large close about it and offices for the officer thereof, and a fine palace for the Bishop.'

(Samuel Pepys (1833–1703))

3.   'I have travelled all over Europe in search of architecture, and I have seen nothing like this.'

(Augustus Pugin (1812–52) looking at the cathedral from the north-east corner of the Close)

4.   'Salisbury is all-glorious without, Westminster [Abbey] is all-glorious within.'

(Arthur Stanley, Dean of Westminster (1815–81))

5.   '... Salisbury's soaring spire, with its graceful, arrowlike rise into the air, gives a special character to the view that makes it, in my opinion, the finest in England.'

(J.J. Hissey, *Through Ten English Counties*, 1894)

6.   '...the most graceful architectural pile in England.'

(Thomas Hardy, writing about 'Melchester' in *Jude the Obscure*, 1895)

7.   '... we looked into the distant vale and saw, far away in the autumnal haze, the spire of Salisbury Cathedral like a pointed finger, faintly luminous. This is a noble view of England and Constable himself could not have contrived a better light for it. You have before you a Shakespearean landscape, with shreds of Arden all about it.'

(W.H. Hudson, *A Shepherd's Life*, 1910)

8.   'I do not remember any cathedral with so fine a site as this, rising up out of the centre of a beautiful green, extensive enough to show its full proportions, relieved and insulated from all other patchwork and impertinence of rusty edifices. It is of gray stone, and looks as perfect as when just finished, and with the perfection, too, that could not have come in less than six centuries of venerableness'.

(Nathaniel Hawthorne (1804–64) from his *English Notebooks*)

9.   'Best of all is the way in which the transition from the square to the octagon was achieved, a problem to which mediaeval builders devoted much thought and plenty of experimentation. Here there are a double tier of pinnacles at each corner and a gabled spire-light, or lucarne, at a lower level in between: a perfect solution. The spire of Salisbury, 404ft high, is loftier by nearly a hundred feet than any other in England; but it is not so much its great height as for its exquisite grace that one may claim for it the supreme place among spires – of any date and in any land. One does not lightly employ the word faultless, but here, for once, it seems to be the *mot juste*.'

(Alec Clifton-Taylor, from *The Cathedrals of England*, 1967)

ELEVEN NOTABLE BISHOPS OF NEW SARUM

Up to the beginning of the twenty-first century there have been seventy-one bishops of Salisbury. Here are eleven of special interest.

1. *Richard Poore* (1217–28), who moved the cathedral to its present site, and who later became Bishop of Durham. On the south wall of the south transept there are memorial tablets to generations of the Poore family – even into the twentieth century. Richard Poore himself is buried at Tarrant Crawford in Dorset, his birthplace.

2. *Giles de Bridport* (1257–62), in whose time the cathedral was consecrated in the presence of King Henry III. He was chosen by the king as one of the arbitrators between himself and the rebellious barons. Giles's tomb, with a curious little monkey carved among the decorations (see page 40), is in the south choir aisle.

3. *Walter de la Wyle* (1263–71), in whose time the cloisters were begun, and who founded St Edmund's Church in Salisbury in memory of Edmund Rich, former treasurer of the cathedral. This church is now in use as a flourishing arts centre.

4. *Robert Wyville* (1330–75), in whose time the Close wall was built when Edward III gave permission for the stone of the old cathedral to be used for that purpose. Wyville's intriguing brass memorial is in the Morning Chapel, and the story of the 'Bishop's Champion' is told on pages 44–5.

5. *Robert Hallam* (1407–17), who was present at the Council of Constance, 1414, and who witnessed the burning of John Hus and Jerome of Prague. A great advocate of church reform.

6. *William Ayscough* (1438–50), Confessor to Henry VI, who officiated at the King's marriage to Margaret of Anjou. He became so unpopular, being associated with the King's misgovernment, that he was murdered in 1450 by the rebel followers of Jack Cade. When Jack Cade himself was killed, a quarter of his corpse was sent to Salisbury to be publicly exhibited there as a warning to would-be rebels.

7. *Lionel Woodville* (1482–4), brother of Edward IV's queen, Elizabeth Woodville, and in whose time the Duke of Buckingham (his brother-in-law) was beheaded in Salisbury marketplace. A plaque noting this execution is on the wall of Debenham's store in Blue Boar Row.

8. *Cardinal Campeggio* (1524–34), bishop before the destruction of the monasteries under Henry VIII. He was appointed to hear the bitter divorce suit of Henry VIII against Catherine of Aragon. After this, Wolsey was disgraced and Campeggio was flung out of office. He died in Rome in 1539.

9. *Seth Ward* (1667–89), former Professor of Astronomy at Oxford, a friend of Sir Christopher Wren, and a founder member of the Royal Society. He asked Wren to survey and strengthen the cathedral, and he built the beautiful 'College of Matrons' just inside the Close, entering from the High Street Gate.

10. *Gilbert Burnet* (1689–1715), friend of King William III, and author of a detailed history of England in the late seventeenth and early eighteenth centuries.

11. *John Wordsworth* (1885–1911), a scholar of international fame, Fellow of Brasenose College, Oxford, and Oriel Professor in the University of Oxford. He was the great-nephew of the poet William Wordsworth. In 1890, at a cost of £3,000, entirely at his own expense, he founded Bishop Wordsworth's School in Salisbury. 'I should like to found a school which shall be equal to the greatest and best of our public schools,' he said. He was also responsible for raising the money to build three new primary schools in the city. His striking effigy in white marble lies on the north side of the Trinity Chapel.

Statue of Bishop Richard Poore on the West Front of the cathedral, the second statue from the left, in the lowest tier of statues. He holds a model of the cathedral as it was when he founded it, without the tower and spire. Next to him, in order, are statues of Henry III, St Edmund of Canterbury and Bishop Odo of Ramsbury. The statue on the left is of an unidentified prelate.

EIGHT WICKED ACTS OF VANDALISM

In 1789 the fashionable architect James Wyatt was asked to 'restore' Salisbury Cathedral. Catastrophically for Salisbury, he set about the task with ferocious energy and wreaked havoc on everything he touched. His nicknames include 'Wyatt the Destroyer' and 'Wyatt the Vandal'.

He had previously designed 'gothick' fantasies such as the country house he built for William Beckford at Fonthill. His 'improvements' of Salisbury Cathedral were perpetrated at the behest of Bishop Shute Barrington, Bishop of Salisbury 1782–91, who hoped to tidy up the cathedral and Close after a period of neglect.

The cathedral has never recovered from James Wyatt's wicked acts of vandalism. They were:

1. The beautiful old bell tower was completely demolished and removed. It stood just at the end of the path leading from the north porch to the road. True, it was unsafe, but it could easily have been strengthened. The outline of this bell tower can still be seen in the lawn of the Close, particularly during a long period of drought, when the grass over the foundations shows a different colour. It is best seen from the cathedral tower.

2. Two fifteenth-century 'Chantries', the Beauchamp Chapel and the Hungerford Chapel, were demolished at the eastern end of the cathedral. They had been built onto the eastern ends of the choir aisles. These were beautiful in themselves, as shown in old prints, but arguably they cluttered up the original simplicity of the cathedral, so Wyatt ruthlessly got rid of them.

3. In destroying the Beauchamp Chapel, built in memory of Richard Beauchamp, Bishop of Salisbury 1450–61, Wyatt somehow mislaid the good bishop's tomb. Beauchamp's remains now lie in an unmarked spot in the nave.

4. Wyatt's idea of getting everything neat and tidy included the removal of all the monuments from their original places in the cathedral, and placing them in orderly rows in the nave.

5. Wyatt whitewashed the vaulted ceilings so that the medieval colourings were covered over.

6. In order to let in more light, he took out all the beautiful thirteenth-century stained glass, replaced it with clear glass and threw the original stained glass into the city's rubbish tip.

7. Wyatt pulled out the choir fittings that Sir Christopher Wren had designed over a century before and threw them away.

8. He destroyed the lovely thirteenth-century stone screen that had been built between the choir and the nave.

ONE SUPERB IMPROVEMENT

James Wyatt may justly be described as 'the Vandal', but there is one piece of work he created that is indescribably beautiful, but for which he seldom receives credit. However, praise should be given where praise is due.

It is to Wyatt that we owe the green and spacious lawn surrounding the cathedral. Everyone who sees the Close is struck by its tranquil loveliness, so it is something of a surprise to know that before Wyatt transformed it in the late eighteenth century it had been 'dirty and neglected as a cow-common', as one visitor described it.

Before Wyatt's improvement there had been small ditches, 'foul and stinking', running through the Close, and a larger 'boggy ditch' stagnating in the centre. Amid all this were decrepit old tombstones around which cattle grazed. Wyatt drained the Close, raised it, covered up the graves and levelled the ground into its present state.

A century later Thomas Hardy was to express his passionate delight in the cathedral and Close. In one of his letters he wrote:

> 'Went into the Close late at night. The moon was visible through both the north and south clerestory windows to me standing on the turf on the north side . . . Walked to the West Front, and watched the moonlight creep round upon the statuary of the façade – stroking tentatively and more and more firmly the prophets, the martyrs, the bishops, the kings, and the queens . . .
>
> Upon the whole, the Close of Salisbury, under the full summer moon on a windless midnight, is as beautiful a scene as any I know in England.'

Thomas Hardy's own sketch of the cathedral interior, showing Sir Gilbert Scott's screen (now removed).

SIX SHORTER SPIRES

It is a well-known fact that Salisbury's spire is the tallest in England, at 404ft. However, the tallest spire in the world is that of Ulm, in Germany, at 530ft. Old St Paul's, in London, which was destroyed in the Great Fire of 1666, originally had a magnificent spire of about 520ft. The cross on the top of the present St Paul's Cathedral, built by Sir Christopher Wren, is 365ft from the pavement.

For comparison, here is a list of six spires that are shorter than Salisbury's.

	Salisbury Cathedral	404ft	(123.139m)
1.	Chartres Cathedral, France	371ft	(113.08m)
2.	St Patrick's Cathedral, New York	328ft	(99.974m)
3.	Norwich Cathedral	315ft	(96.012m)
4.	Chichester Cathedral	277ft	(84.430m)
5.	St Mary's Cathedral, Edinburgh	275ft	(83.82m)
6.	Lichfield Cathedral, central spire	258ft	(78.688m)

FIVE TALLER BUILDINGS

Modern engineering techniques enable architects to construct buildings that are astonishingly tall. Salisbury's spire is dwarfed by the following structures.

1.	Sears Tower, Chicago, USA	1,453ft	(443m)
2.	Empire State Building, New York	1,249ft	(381m)
3.	Eiffel Tower, Paris	984ft	(300m)
4.	The London Telecom Tower	580ft	(176m)
5.	The London Eye	450ft	(137m)
	Salisbury Cathedral	404ft	(123.139m)

SIXTY BIBLICAL SCENES CARVED IN STONE

One of the most fascinating features in the cathedral is the vibrant set of medieval carvings around the tops of the arches in the Chapter House, ingeniously fitting into the V-shaped gaps. It is a test of our knowledge of the first books of the Bible. Here is a checklist of what they all are.

1. God creates light
2. God creates the firmament
3. Creation of trees
4. Creation of the sun and moon
5. Creation of the birds and fishes
6. Creation of beasts and Adam and Eve
7. God rests on the seventh day
8. God shows Adam the tree of good and evil
9. Adam and Eve eating fruit of the tree
10. God speaks to Adam and Eve, who are hiding
11. The expulsion from Eden
12. Eve nursing and Adam working
13. Sacrifice of Cain and Abel
14. Cain murders Abel
15. God sentences Cain
16. God commands Noah to build the Ark
17. Noah enters the Ark; he receives the dove
18. Noah prunes his vineyard
19. The drunkenness of Noah
20. Building the tower of Babel
21. Abraham asks the three angels to stay
22. Abraham waits on the angels at table
23. Destruction of Sodom and Gomorrah
24. Lot leaves Sodom; the pillar of salt
25. Abraham takes Isaac to sacrifice
26. Abraham about to sacrifice Isaac
27. Isaac blesses Jacob
28. Isaac blesses Esau
29. Rebecca sends Jacob to Padan-Aram
30. Jacob removes the stone from the well
31. Rachel brings Jacob to Laban
32. Jacob and angel wrestle; ladder of angels
33. The angel touches Jacob's thigh
34. Reunion of Jacob and Esau
35. Joseph's dreams
36. Joseph relates his dream
37. Joseph is cast into the pit
38. Joseph is sold and taken away
39. Joseph's coat is shown to Jacob
40. Pharaoh receives Joseph
41. Joseph is tempted by Potiphar's wife
42. Joseph is accused before Pharaoh
43. Joseph is imprisoned with the butler and baker
44. The baker is hanged; the butler gives Pharaoh a cup
45. Pharaoh's dream
46. Pharaoh with a magician and the butler
47. Joseph is presented to Pharaoh
48. Joseph supervises the corn threshing
49. Joseph's brothers fill the sacks
50. Benjamin presented to Joseph; a cup
51. The cup is found in Benjamin's sack
52. Joseph is recognised by his brothers and he embraces Benjamin
53. Jacob and his family go to Egypt
54. The family meet Joseph
55. Jacob and Joseph embrace
56. Moses and the burning bush
57. Passage of the Red Sea
58. Destruction of Pharaoh's army
59. Moses strikes the rock
60. God gives the law to Moses

It is also well worth noticing the curious heads and other decorations just below the main carvings – especially the little monkey hidden in foliage in the north-east corner.

Three biblical scenes in the Chapter House frieze.

(45) Pharaoh's dream.
(49) Joseph's brothers fill the sacks.
(54) The family meets Joseph.

This is an engraving made in 1815 showing the dilapidated state of the carvings at that time. Parliamentarian commissioners had used the Chapter House for their meetings during the Civil War, and much damage was done. The carvings were restored in 1855 by John Birnie Philip, who was later to carve many of the figures on the Albert Memorial. This engraving has taken some artistic liberties and shows three scenes that are not adjacent to one another in the frieze itself. Interestingly, the scene showing Pharaoh's dream was the only one to escape Cromwellian damage. The scene of Noah's ark (shown below) almost escaped damage; only the dove and the raven's foot were broken.

High Street Gate, looking into the Close. This fourteenth-century gate once had a portcullis to protect the bishop and clergy from threats and attack by rebellious citizens. In the 1640s, during the Civil War, the royal arms were torn down, but the Stuart royal coat of arms was put back in place at the restoration of Charles II in 1660.

SIX HOUSES IN THE CLOSE AS YOU ENTER THROUGH THE HIGH STREET GATE

Many visitors arrive at the Close through the High Street Gate. Here are the main buildings in the order in which you reach them as you walk towards the cathedral. (R and L indicate whether to look right or left as you walk along the road.)

No. 48 (R)   The Porter's Lodge. The office of Porter is important, especially as the Close is closed at 11.00 every night and latecomers have to knock for admittance. The Close Constable still officiates.

Nos. 39–46 (L)   This is the graceful long building with the arms of Charles II over the main doorway. It is known as the College of Matrons, and was built in 1682 by Bishop Seth Ward as a home for widows and unmarried daughters of clergy. Seth Ward had been Professor of Mathematics at Oxford and was a member of the Royal Society. He invited Christopher Wren, a friend and former pupil, to give advice on the strengthening of the cathedral tower and spire. The style of this 'College' is typical of Wren, but the architect was Alexander Fort.

The College of Matrons, 1682, built by Bishop Seth Ward, showing the royal coat of arms.

Turn right and walk along the road bordering a grass square known as the Green. The most important building overlooking the Green is on your right.

No. 53 (R)   Mompesson House, built in the late seventeenth century, begun by Sir Thomas Mompesson, MP for Salisbury, and completed by his son, Charles Mompesson, in 1701. It is one of the most beautiful houses in the Close, and is now owned by the National Trust. Its eighteenth-century elegance makes it well worth a visit.

Mompesson House, as seen from Choristers' Green.

No. 56 (R)   Tucked into the north-west corner of the Close, No. 56 is easy to miss. It is called Hemingsby, after the earliest recorded resident, Canon Hemingsby, who died in 1334. The house itself dates back to the fourteenth century and it incorporates some tiles from Old Sarum. A later occupant, Canon Fideon, had escaped from Constantinople when it had been captured by the Turks in 1453. And a still later occupant, Canon Edward Powell, had the courage to refuse to agree with Henry VIII over his divorce from Catherine of Aragon. Powell was taken to the Tower of London in 1534, held prisoner for six years, and was hanged, drawn and quartered for being a traitor.

Hemingsby in the north-west corner of the Close consists of two buildings adjoining one another.

Turn left, and walk along, with the Green on your left.

No. 56 (R)   Although this is called Wren Hall, it has no connection with Sir Christopher Wren. It was built in 1715 as a new grammar school for the cathedral choirboys. It may be visited, and the old schoolmaster's desk can still be seen at the end of the room. The boys played games on the Green, and at one time cows grazed there, useful to provide the boys with milk.

Wren Hall

No. 58 (R)   Known as the Wardrobe, this is now the Regimental Headquarters and Museum of the Duke of Edinburgh's Royal Regiment. The house dates back to the thirteenth century. It was built as a canon's house, and later used by the bishop as a storeroom and 'wardrobe' – hence its name. It is well worth visiting.

Harnham Gate, leading out of the Close towards the south. The College of St Nicholas de Vaux is just beyond this exit from the Close.

SEVEN HOUSES IN THE CLOSE OPPOSITE THE WEST FRONT OF THE CATHEDRAL

The most interesting houses in the Close are those facing the West Front of the cathedral.

No. 59 — Known as Arundells, this elegant eighteenth-century house is the home of the former Prime Minister, Sir Edward Heath. A previous occupant, Canon Alderson, nephew of another former Prime Minister, Lord Salisbury, was always eager to receive visitors, and reminded his faithful friends that its number, 59, was that of the hymn 'O Come, all ye Faithful' in *Hymns Ancient and Modern*.

No. 59 – Arundells.

No. 60 — The North Canonry dates from the thirteenth century and is almost as old as the cathedral itself, although it was altered in the sixteenth and seventeenth centuries. On special occasions this is open to visitors. The twentieth-century buildings next to the North Canonry once housed the College of Sarum St Michael, a training college for women teachers. (This college formerly occupied the King's House, which is the next building along the road.)

Medieval Hall — Go up the entrance drive beside the south side of the North Canonry and turn left, and you will soon come to what is now called the Medieval Hall – in fact it was the Great Hall of the original Deanery, built in about 1220, where the Deans would entertain their guests to feasts and banquets. Nowadays it has been turned into a fascinating museum, with a continuous showing of a documentary about the history of Salisbury city and cathedral. Visitors may find refreshment and entertainment, and it is frequently booked for dinners and receptions. See page 112 for further details.

THE CATHEDRAL ORGANIST TRIED TO MURDER THE DEAN

In 1592 a notorious scandal took place in the Old Deanery (now the Medieval Hall), involving John Farrant, the cathedral organist. Farrant was a hot-tempered man, and took great offence when his father-in-law – Dean Bridges – began to interfere in his domestic affairs. Farrant quietly left the cathedral in the middle of evensong, went to the Deanery, entered the Dean's study, and tried to stab his father-in-law to death. Luckily, the Dean managed to escape to his bedroom. Foiled in his attempt to murder the Dean, Farrant went back to the cathedral and loyally resumed singing his part in the evening anthem! Not surprisingly, he was dismissed from his post.

No. 65   This is the King's House, so named because James I often came to stay here with his friend Thomas Sadler, who was then its owner. Before the dissolution of the monasteries, this house was the official residence of the Abbots of Sherborne whenever they came to stay in Salisbury, so it was then called Sherborne Place. The main part of the house dates from the fifteenth century, but Sadler built the right wing in 1598. General George Henry Shrapnel, inventor of shrapnel shell, lived here in the eighteenth century. In the nineteenth century the King's House became a training college for women teachers, and Thomas Hardy's sisters were students here. Hardy brought this college into *Jude the Obscure*, where Sue Bridehead came to study. The King's House now contains the Salisbury and South Wiltshire Museum – an essential part of any sightseeing visit to Salisbury (see pages 100–1).

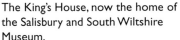

The King's House, now the home of the Salisbury and South Wiltshire Museum.

No. 68   Myles Place, built in about 1720, was named after a sixteenth-century cleric, and has been described as 'the most stately eighteenth-century house in the Close'. Sir Arthur Bryant, the historian, lived here for almost forty years until his death in 1985.

No. 69   The Walton Canonry, built in about 1719, was named after Canon Isaak Walton, son of the famous Isaak Walton who wrote *The Compleat Angler*, published in 1653, and also various biographies, including a *Life of George Herbert*, who had lived in Bemerton on the outskirts of Salisbury (see page 92). The artist Rex Whistler and the author Leslie Thomas have also lived in this house.

The Walton Canonry.

No. 70   This is Leadenhall, where John Constable stayed when he was painting his well-known pictures of Salisbury Cathedral. Constable was a friend of the Archdeacon, John Fisher. Leadenhall is built on the site of an earlier *Aula plumbea* (Latin for 'Leadenhall'), which was probably so named because of its lead roof. The Leadenhall we see today was built in 1717.

Above: Leadenhall.

Below: Exterior of south side of cloisters.

Right: A glimpse of the cathedral workshops.

Then, if you walk on, turn left and follow this road eastwards towards the cathedral cloisters, you will reach the workshops where skilled craftsmen constantly work at repairing and restoring the fabric of the cathedral, in stone, wood and glass.

NINE HOUSES IN THE CLOSE AS YOU ENTER THROUGH ST ANN'S GATE

If you enter the Close by St Ann's Gate, the following houses are to be seen. (R and L indicate whether to look right or left as you walk towards the cathedral.)

Malmesbury House (R)	Malmesbury House is just inside the gate – in fact the gate is built into it. The house is named after James Harris, First Earl of Malmesbury, and was owned by three James Harrises – father, son and grandson. It was the grandson who was rewarded by the earldom, because of his diplomatic services. The family were great patrons of the arts, especially music, and it was at the invitation of the second James Harris that Handel came and gave his first public concert in England in the room above St Ann's Gate, which is a part of Malmesbury House. Note the sundial on the side of the house, dated 1749, with its quotation from *Macbeth* – 'Life's but a walking shadow.' Malmesbury House is open to visitors at certain times.
No. 14 (L)	Henry Fielding stayed in this house writing his novel *Tom Jones*, published in 1749. The house belonged to his mother-in-law, Mrs Craddock.
No. 11 (L)	This was acquired shortly after the Second World War by Bishop Wordsworth's School for use as sixth-form classrooms. At that time William Golding was one of the schoolmasters who taught there, and it is said that he used school exercise books in which to write his famous novel, *Lord of the Flies*. He used to sing in the school choir – possibly the source of inspiration for this book. A few years later he wrote *The Spire* – a novel obviously based on Salisbury Cathedral.
No. 19 (R)	The main building was built in the seventeenth century, and formerly housed a theological college.

At this point you may turn left and go down Bishop's Walk.

No. 7 (L)	The Deanery was built in the seventeenth century by a Francis Sambrook, who then added what is now No. 6 as his kitchens.
No. 6 (L)	This is the office of the Dean and Chapter.
No. 5 (L)	This is the house of the cathedral organist, the front of which was built in 1747, though the rear part dates back to medieval times, when the cathedral choirboys were taught here in a 'song school'.

If you continue to the end of Bishop's Walk, you can catch a glimpse of the medieval Bishop's Palace, which is nowadays used as the boarding school for the choristers. Then retrace your steps back to the main road, North Walk.

No. 21 (R)	This house has a curious name – Aula le Stage – because in the fifteenth century it possessed a small tower. Thus it had a third storey or 'stage'. The original house dates back to the thirteenth century, shortly after the cathedral itself was built. It was rebuilt by Thomas Bennett, acting Dean of the Cathedral during the reign of Henry VIII. *Aula* is Latin for a forecourt, cattle-yard, inner court or hall – but it is unclear which of these meanings applies to Aula de Stage.

FIVE HUNDRED MILLION TICKS

The old clock situated in the north aisle near the north porch door claims its place in *The Guinness Book of Records* as having ticked more than 500 million times – but this statistic increases every second! Here are the essential facts.

1. Made in or before 1386, this is the earliest mechanical clock in working order in the world. It was made at the time that Chaucer was writing his *Canterbury Tales*.

2. The bishop at this time was Ralph Erghum. He moved from Salisbury to the see of Bath and Wells in 1388, and in 1392 another clock was recorded as existing in Wells Cathedral. It is almost certain that the same craftsman made them both.

3. Both clocks are made entirely of hand-wrought iron.

4. Strangely, compared with modern clocks, neither of these had a dial.

5. The Salisbury clock struck only the hours: the Wells clock also struck the quarters. Obviously the clockmaker was getter better at his trade.

6. The Salisbury clock was originally placed in the old bell tower, which was pulled down in 1790. It needed a new home . . .

7. . . . so after 1790 it was placed in the central tower of the cathedral.

8. It was in use until 1884, when it was pensioned off following the installation of a new clock.

9. In 1929 it was inspected, and declared to be the oldest clock in the world. In 1931 it was set up in the north transept – not, however, in working order.

10. In 1956 it was completely repaired and restored to its original condition and placed in its present position in the north aisle of the nave.

Salisbury Cathedral's ancient clock.

THREE UNFLATTERING COMMENTS
ABOUT THE CATHEDRAL

Not every visitor has agreed that Salisbury Cathedral is attractive. To keep a balanced view, here are three damning remarks – some made by well-known writers.

1. 'Salisbury is a little old city, very ugly and of which there is nothing to say, except that the steeple of its cathedral, which is immensely high and built of stone to its very summit, is 20 inches out of the perpendicular, which is enough to take off the attention of the most devout congregation. We went to those officiating. It is not the first time we have observed this desertion of the metropolitan churches – even where the steeples were quite perpendicular.'

    (An unknown French visitor in 1810)

2. 'I confess that on repeated inspection it [the spire] grew to seem to me the least bit banal, or even bête, since I am talking French, and I began to consider whether it does not belong to the same range of art as the Apollo Belvedere or the Venus de'Medici. I am inclined to think that if I had to live within sight of a cathedral and encounter it in my daily comings and goings I should grow less weary of the rugged black front of Exeter than of the sweet perfection of Salisbury. There are people by temperament easily sated with beauties specifically fair, and the effect of Salisbury Cathedral architecturally is equivalent to that of flaxen hair and blue eyes physiognomically.'

    (Henry James, *English Hours*, 1905)

3. 'Occasionally I met and talked with an old man employed at the cathedral. One day, closing one eye and shading the other with his hand, he gazed up at the building for some time, and then remarked: "I'll tell you what's wrong with Salisbury – it looks too noo." He was near the mark; the fault is that to the professional eye it is faultless; the lack of expression is due to the fact that it came complete from its maker's brain, like a coin from the mint, and being all in one symmetrical plan it has the trim, neat appearance of a toy cathedral carved out of wood and set on a green-painted square.'

    (W.H. Hudson, *Afoot in England*, 1909)

'... enough to take off the attention of the most devout congregation'.

FOURTEEN FACTS ABOUT SALISBURY'S PATRON SAINT

For almost three and a half centuries Osmund was venerated as a saint even before he became officially canonised. His cult brought thousands of pilgrims into the city. Today, a candle burns perpetually in the Trinity Chapel in his memory. These are some of the facts.

1. Osmund was born in Normany, the son of Henry, Count of Séez, and a relation of William the Conqueror.

2. In 1066 he accompanied William the Conqueror in the invasion of England. Osmund may have fought at the Battle of Hastings. He became royal chaplain and was created Earl of Dorset.

3. In 1072 he was promoted to be Chancellor, thus becoming the most important man in England under the Conqueror.

4. In 1078 he succeeded Herman as bishop of Salisbury – that is, Old Sarum – and he completed and consecrated the old cathedral.

5. He was a popular bishop, and helped to reconcile the Saxons and Normans. He initiated the Sarum Rite (the Use of Sarum), which became a model of worship for other English cathedrals. He collected a fine library for the cathedral.

6. As bishop he was still an active administrator, and helped to prepare the Domesday Book for William the Conqueror.

7. He died in 1099 and was buried in the old cathedral. Miracles immediately began to occur at his tomb (see the next page), and he was popularly regarded as a saint.

8. In 1226 his body and its tomb were brought into the new cathedral.

9. Attempts were made to canonise Osmund in 1228, 1387 and 1406, but it was not until 1456 that Osmund was finally declared to be a saint.

10. In 1457 a new shrine was set up in the Trinity Chapel in Salisbury Cathedral and Henry VI came to pray at his tomb and add to its sumptuous decoration.

11. He was regarded as a saint to be prayed to especially by sufferers of toothache, rupture, paralysis and madness.

12. In 1534 his shrine was destroyed on the orders of Henry VIII, who forbade the worship of saints.

13. His tomb was moved to the nave during the 'improvements' of James Wyatt.

14. In 1999, on the 900th anniversary of his death, Osmund's tomb was brought back into the Trinity Chapel again, where it has originally been placed, and the marble top was placed in the centre of this chapel, where it is once again in a place of honour.

EIGHT SAINTLY MIRACLES

When Osmund was canonised in 1456, fifty-two miracles were claimed to have taken place at his tomb, attested by seventy-five witnesses. Here is a selection.

1. Agnes, a girl of fourteen, fell on a hot spit of wood that pierced right through her body. Her mother was convinced she would die, but after prayers had been said in the name of St Osmund she recovered well enough to go to the saint's tomb and give thanks.

2. Christina, a girl from Laverstock, was hit on the head by an iron quoit. She fell to the ground unconscious for an hour and a half. Prayers to St Osmund restored her to health.

3. A boy who fell on a knife was believed to be dead, but the power of Osmund brought him back to life again.

4. William Hendyng of Laverstock had lost the sight of his right eye having been caught in a thorn bush. Osmund healed his eye and he could see again.

5. A man with a diseased jaw could no longer speak or eat. As he prayed at Osmund's tomb, the decayed bone fell away and was replaced by a healthy one.

6. Numerous cases of toothache being cured led to Osmund becoming a patron saint for sufferers of toothache.

7. A drowned child was restored to life.

8. A man from Bemerton was on a pilgrimage in the Holy Land. A lady appeared to him in a vision and handed him a letter for the Bishop of Salisbury. She touched him and he fell asleep. On waking, he found himself back in Salisbury!

St Osmund's Tomb, now on the south side of the Trinity Chapel.

A COLLECTION OF HALF-HIDDEN ANIMALS

Challenge your children to find these animals and mythical creatures as they look round the cathedral. The first five items are in the Chapter House.

1.   *A monkey* is to be found at the top of a column in the Chapter House, just beneath one of the carvings of Noah's Ark.

2.   *A dove* and various indeterminate animals are shown in the ark's windows. The dove is on the right, bringing an olive branch in its beak.

3.   *Birds, fishes and beasts* are depicted, as God is shown creating all kinds of creatures during the first six days of creation.

4.   *A snake with a woman's head and face* (depicting the Devil) can be seen coiled round the tree of good and evil. It has the face of a deceitful woman.

5.   *A pony, cattle, a horse and a ram* are all to be found in the many sculptures telling the Bible stories round the Chapter House.

6.   *Three rabbits* are depicted at the bottom of the brass to Bishop Wyville in the Morning Chapel – which leads from the north choir aisle. These rabbits specifically refer to the Chase of Bere, which was well known for its huge rabbit warren (see pages 44–5).

7.   *A mole* is carved at the feet of the figure of Thomas Bennett, whose tomb is almost opposite the door into the Morning Chapel, at the rear of the choir stalls. Thomas Bennett is shown as a gruesome 'cadaver' or corpse, and the mole is shown burrowing into the earth where he is laid.

8.   *A whale* can be found on the pulpit, reminding us of the story of Jonah.

9.   *A cricket* is also to be found on the pulpit.

10.   *A griffon* forms an arm-rest at the rear of the choir stalls on the north side.

11.   *A beaver* is to be found on another arm-rest near the griffon, also on the north side of the choir stalls. This is particularly interesting, because beavers were hunted to extinction in England in the thirteenth century. As these choir stalls were carved in the thirteenth century, it is likely that the carver actually saw an English beaver before they became extinct.

12.   *A lion* is at the feet of Sir John Montacute, whose memorial is on the north side of the nave. For an explanation of this lion's significance see page 61.

13.   *A dog* is at the feet of Lord Robert Hungerford, whose memorial is on the south side of the nave.

14.   *Another monkey* is an intriguing carving on the tomb of Bishop Giles de Bridport, who was the bishop when the cathedral was consecrated in 1258. His monument is in the south choir aisle, and the monkey is on the top, at the right-hand end. The monkey is holding a nut in its hand – and an old story tells that it will mischievously throw it at anyone who strokes his nose !

15.   *A warty toad* is carved in the back row of the choir stalls on the north side.

The toad (back row of the
north side of the choir).

THREE CURIOUS REBUSES

Rebus is Latin for 'with things'. In earlier centuries, when many people could not read, the names of persons or places were sometimes depicted by means of 'things' – pictures of objects that, if said aloud, resembled the sound of that name. For example, a man named 'Appleton' could be depicted by a picture of an apple and a barrel (or 'tun'). Here are three curious rebuses to be found on memorials in Salisbury Cathedral.

1. *'Pointed mountains' for Sir John de Montacute, 'King of the Isle of Man'.* Sir John's monument is on the north side of the nave (see page 61), and on the ends of his stone memorial are coats of arms showing three diamond shapes with sharp points rising upwards. In heraldic terms these are known as 'fusils'. Each of these points can be regarded as a mountain top, or *mons acutus*. This referred to a steep hill in France from where the 'Monacute' family originated.

2. *'Hedgehogs' for James Harris.* The memorial to James Harris, first Earl of Malmesbury, is in the north transept, and the Harris coat of arms carved on this memorial shows three hedgehogs. The old spelling of the name 'Harris' was 'Herries' – and the French word for hedgehog is hérisson. The heraldic term for a hedgehog is also 'herison'.

3. A *'cockerel' for Sir Walter Alcock.* One of England's most distinguished organists was Sir Walter Alcock, organist of Salisbury Cathedral for thirty-one years, from 1916 until his death in 1947. He had the honour of playing the organ in Westminster Abbey for three coronation services: for those of Edward VII, George V and George VI. As he was asked for his ticket to get into Westminster Abbey for the third of these, he simply replied: 'Season!' and walked in. In the south aisle of the choir, on the wooden screen of the organ, there is a memorial plaque to Sir Walter. It shows a cockerel ('Alcock' more or less said backwards).

'Fusils' representing 'pointed mountains' on the eastern end of the monument of Sir John Montacute.

SEVEN HERALDIC SHIELDS IN THE WEST WINDOW

The three large windows of the great West Front contain a variety of pieces of glass, placed into their present design by John Beare, another local glazier, between 1819 and 1824. Some of these pieces were found in London; others were retrieved from elsewhere. The seven heraldic shields along the bottom of the west window were originally in the Chapter House.

These shields have special interest, as being some of the oldest stained glass in the cathedral. The formal heraldic descriptions given below are in italics, followed by an everyday 'translation' in roman type. They are listed from left to right.

1. Gilbert de Clare, Earl of Gloucester (1262–95). *Or three chevrons gules* (three red 'arrows' pointing upwards, on a golden background)

2. Unknown.

3. Eleanor of Provence (1222–91), wife of Henry III. *Paly gules and or* (red and gold vertical stripes). Queen Eleanor was present at the consecration of Salisbury Cathedral in 1258.

4. France – arms of King Louis IX, brother-in-law of Queen Eleanor. *Azure powdered with fleur de lys or* (lots of golden fleur-de-lys on a blue background)

5. England – arms of Henry III (reigned 1216–72). *Gules three leopards passant gardant or* (three golden lions on a red background). Henry III was a generous patron of Salisbury Cathedral, which was built during his long reign. He attended its consecration in 1258. The arms shown here are particularly interesting, as they are the old arms of England during the reigns of Richard I, John, Henry III, Edward I and Edward II.

6. Richard, Earl of Cornwall, brother of Henry III (1225–72). *Argent a lion rampant gules crowned or within a bezanty border sable* (a red lion with a golden crown standing with a silver background and surrounded by a black border decorated with circles.) 'Bezanty' is derived from the name of a Byzantine golden coin, the 'bezant', which appear in the heraldic arms of Cornwall.

7. Roger Bigod, Earl of Norfolk and Earl Marshall (1226–70). *Or a cross gules* (a red cross on a golden background).

As a modern contrast, this is a detail from a stained-glass window in the north aisle, made in 1949 and depicting those who fought and served in the Second World War. It shows a landgirl and a member of the Auxiliary Territorial Services (now the Women's Royal Army Corps).

AN EIGHTEENTH-CENTURY GLAZIER SMASHES UP THE CATHEDRAL'S STAINED-GLASS WINDOWS

The vandalism perpetrated at the time of James Wyatt's 'restoration' of the cathedral in the late eighteenth century can be judged by this illiterate letter, dated 1788, written by John Berry, glazier of Salisbury, to a Mr Lloyd of Conduit Street, London:

Sir,

This day I have sent you a Box full of old Staind & Painted Glass, as you desired me to due, wich I hope will sute your Purpos, it his the best that I can get at present. But I expect to Beat to Peceais a very great deale verey sune, as it his of nowe use to we, and we Due it for the lead if yow want Eney more of the same sorts you may have what thear is, if it will Pay for Taking out, as it is a Deal of Truble to what Beating it to Peceais his. You will send me a line as soon as Posobl, for we are goain to move ore glasing shop to a Nother plase, and thin we hope to save a great deale more of the like sort.

Which I ham your most Omble servant –

JOHN BERRY

Three of the stained-glass shields described on the opposite page. Arms of Eleanor of France. Arms of King Louis IX of France. Arms of King Henry III of England. Luckily, these shields managed to survive the vandalism of James Wyatt and John Berry.

Bishop Wyville's brass memorial in the Morning Chapel, showing his champion at the gate of Sherborne Castle. There are three rabbits in the grass at his feet.

PADDED WITH PRAYERS TO FIGHT FOR A
RABBIT WARREN

On the floor of the Morning Chapel on the north side of the choir is a fascinating large brass memorial to Bishop Wyville. Three little rabbits are to be found popping in and out of their burrows at the foot of this brass.

The engraving looks confusing at first, but you soon realise that it represents four concentric walls of a castle. It is Sherborne Castle, and standing in the middle, with his hands folded in prayer and his mitre on his head, is Bishop Wyville. Boldly in front of him, outside the portcullis gate, is his 'Champion', ready to do battle on his behalf.

The story behind this brass is that Robert Wyville, Bishop of Salisbury 1330–75, was determined to regain Sherborne Castle and an estate known as the Chase of Bere, which had been confiscated from a previous bishop – Bishop Roger – by King Henry I in the early twelfth century. It was now nearly two and a half centuries later, and the monarch on the throne was King Edward III.

Much to Bishop Wyville's annoyance, Edward III had decided to give Sherborne Castle and the Chase of Bere to William Montacute, Earl of Salisbury. At first, Bishop Wyville offered to buy them from the Earl, but the Earl stubbornly refused to listen, and rather alarmingly declared that the issue should be settled by single combat.

Obviously the Bishop and the Earl could not be expected to battle it out in person, so each of them appointed a 'Champion'. The Bishop's Champion, shown here on the brass, is Richard Shawell, and he duly prepared for mortal combat while Bishop Wyville ordered special masses and prayers to be said for him. Intriguingly, when his armour was inspected by the judges just before the contest, his suit was found to be padded with pieces of parchment, with prayers written on them!

Tension must have been acute as bishop and earl prepared for battle. However, at the last moment Edward III decided that things had got out of hand, and ordered the contest to be abandoned, declaring that the Bishop should pay 2,500 marks for Sherborne Castle and 500 marks for the Chase of Bere.

The Chase of Bere was famed for its gigantic rabbit warren (rabbits were a useful source of food in those days), so this is the reason why the rabbits were engraved on the Bishop's memorial.

Bishop Wyville is also to be remembered for having persuaded Edward III to allow the stone from Old Sarum to be used for the building of the Close wall and gateways. Moreover, it was during his time as bishop that the cathedral spire was built.

FOUR UNIQUE WORKS OF ART IN GLASS

Salisbury Cathedral possesses four exquisite works by Laurence Whistler (1912–2000), displaying his genius as a glass engraver. Laurence Whistler lived near Salisbury and revived this rare art form, which had almost died out.

1. *The Rex Whistler Prism.* The most important of Laurence Whistler's works in the cathedral is set in the west wall of the Morning Chapel. It is a memorial to his brother Rex (1905–44), the well-known artist, book illustrator and stage designer. The illuminated prism is 15in high, perpetually revolving and successively revealing three illuminated images of the cathedral. The image reproduced on this page shows the spire soaring into the clouds; the second shows the nave; and the third depicts the geometric vault of the Chapter House. As a work of art, it is unique.

2 & 3. *The Booker Panels.* It's easy to miss these glass panels, for they are mounted on the back of the organ case in the north choir aisle, in an area that is not particularly well lit. They are memorials to two sisters, Joanna and Serena Booker, both of whom died young: Joanna was only thirty-seven, and Serena was tragically murdered in Thailand aged twenty-eight.

   The left-hand panel, with the yew tree, shows the Stour valley with the girls' childhood home and the church of St Nicholas, Durweston, where they are buried. The right-hand panel shows a view of Hambledon with the river Stour – the 'river of life'. Both panels contain quotations from T.S. Eliot's great poem, *Four Quartets.*

4. *The Sydney Evans Bowl.* Sydney Evans, Dean of Salisbury 1977–88, is remembered for enriching the cathedral in many ways, not least for bringing the *Prisoners of Conscience* window into the building. On his retirement he was presented with a beautiful glass bowl, engraved by Laurence Whistler, which is now on view in the Chapter House.

TWO STONE CORPSES, A SKULL AND A MOLE

Two 'cadaver' effigies are to be found in the north choir aisle, backing onto the choir stalls. Cadavers are gruesome representations of skeletons or corpses, often lying in an open shroud. They were in vogue during the later Middle Ages, especially at the time of Hans Holbein's series of woodcuts, *The Dance of Death*.

1. *Thomas Bennett* (d. 1558). Precentor and Chancellor of the cathedral, Bennett died in 1558, having somehow managed to survive in office during both the Protestant reign of Henry VIII and the Catholic reign of Queen ('Bloody') Mary. He is shown lying in his open shroud, with a skull and a mole at his feet.

2. *Archdeacon Sydenham* (d. 1554). A contemporary of Thomas Bennett, Sydenham had been a chaplain to Henry VIII, Warden of de Vaux College and Archdeacon of Sarum.

The sharply grim message of cadavers is to remind everyone that, however important they may be in life, death will reduce even the proudest person to dust. We shall all be corpses like these.

Carved skull of Thomas Bennett.

Carved skull of Archdeacon Sydenham.

Mole and skull at the feet of Thomas Bennett.

SIX GRIM 'ITEMS OF CORRECTION FOR OFFENDERS'

James I made eight visits to Salisbury. He enjoyed staying in what is now called the King's House in the Close, which now houses the Salisbury Museum. In 1612 King James granted Salisbury a Charter of Incorporation, thus freeing the city from the power of the bishop, a crucially important event in the history of Salisbury. At the same time he gave a separate and independent Charter to the Close. As a part of these provisions, the authorities within the Close were allowed the following grim 'items of correction'.

1.   *Stocks* were set up near the north entrance to the churchyard – probably near to where the *Walking Madonna* is to be found today.

2.   A *whipping-post* with irons on it was set up besides these stocks, 'for correction of offenders'.

3.   A *pillory* was also set up nearby.

4.   A *tumbrel* was kept for the conveyance of offenders.

5.   A *prison*, known as 'le Grate', was incorporated within High Street Gate.

6.   *Gallows* were permanently set up on 'le Busshopes Downe'.

Visitors enjoying the peaceful atmosphere of the Close today can hardly imagine the agonising punishments inflicted on law-breakers in seventeenth-century Salisbury.

Manacles carved on the base of the old City Gaol in Fisherton Street.

FIVE FACTS ABOUT THE CATHEDRAL'S CHOIR

There are about 20 boys and 24 girls in the twenty-first century's co-educational prep school: 16 boy choristers with 4 probationers; and 17 girl choristers with 7 probationers. Anyone attending the sung services at the cathedral will be entranced by the singing of the choir. Perhaps surprisingly to some, the top parts may be sung either by girls or by boys. Salisbury Cathedral can boast that it was the first in the country to found a cathedral girls' choir. Here are some facts about the cathedral's musical traditions.

1. *The first cathedral school* was founded by Bishop Osmund in 1091. In those times it was unthinkable that girls should take part, so the choir was exclusively for boys and men.

2. *The first girls' cathedral choir* was begun in Salisbury In 1991 – exactly nine hundred years later. Since then there have been two choirs: boys and girls practising separately and singing separately.

3. *The boy choristers moved into the Bishop's Palace in 1947.* Before this, they lived and had their school on the west side of 'Choristers' Green', and had their lessons in the Wren Hall.

4. *Today the choristers live in the Old Bishop's Palace.* You can see this from a door in the south-east corner of the cloisters. In former times many kings stayed in this old building. Today it is the choristers' prep school.

5. *There has been a succession of schools* over the centuries: a Norman Grammar School at Old Sarum; a Song School; a City Grammar School; a Free School in the Close; School of the Canons of the Close; the Cathedral School; the Choristers' School. Today's co-educational prep school in the Old Bishop's Palace is probably the most successful of them all.

Teach me, my God and King, In all things thee to see,
And what I do in any-thing To do it as for thee.

Where-fore with my ut-most art I will sing thee,
And the cream of all my heart I will bring thee. ...

Extracts from two hymns; words by George Herbert, 1593–1633.

The West Front of Salisbury Cathedral.

SIXTY-SEVEN STATUES ON THE WEST FRONT

Most of the original statues on the West Front of Salisbury Cathedral have been lost because of weather or deliberate destruction. Sadly, in 1802 only nine medieval statues were left. In 1863 a programme of restoration was begun, and the sculptor James Redfern created many replacements. In the 1990s the West Front and its statues were thoroughly cleaned and renovated, and some new angels were added. Then on 29 May 2000, a great outdoor concert was held in the presence of Charles, Prince of Wales, to celebrate the completion of the West Front restoration. Here is a complete guide to all the statues on the West Front.

Christ in Majesty is at the top, with a symbolic bird above Him – either the DOVE of the Holy Spirit, or possibly the *pelican*, emblem of Christ because of the legend that it feeds its young with blood from its own breast.

The statues below are arranged in five horizontal tiers. We look at each tier from left to right.

1st Tier   *Just below the top parapet.*
Contains 6 archangels and angels.
Archangel carrying globe and sceptre; angel playing a harp; three choral angels; and an archangel carrying a globe is on the far right.

2nd Tier   *On level with the top of the great west window.*
Contains 11 Old Testament patriarchs and prophets.
King David with harp; Moses with 10 commandments; Isaiah; Jeremiah; Ezekiel; Abraham with knife to sacrifice Isaac; Noah with Ark; Job; Daniel with lion; Samuel; King Solomon with sceptre and Temple of Jerusalem.

3rd Tier   *On level with the bottom of the great west window.*
Contains 14 Apostles and Evangelists.
St Jude with halberd; St Simon with saw; St Andrew with cross; St Thomas with carpenter's square; St Peter with keys; then, against the north buttress of the window, St Matthew stands above St Mark; against the south buttress St John the Evangelist stands above St Luke; St Paul with sword; St James the Less with fuller's club; St James the Great with pilgrim's staff; St Bartholomew with knife; and St Matthias with lance.

4th Tier   *On level between the west window and the doorways.*
Contains 25 doctors, martyrs and virgins.
Round the corner on the north side of the cathedral is St Patrick, Patron Saint of Ireland, with a snake beneath his feet, as he exterminated snakes from Ireland. Starting at the extreme left of the West Front: St Ambrose of Milan with scourge and staff; St Jerome with Cardinal's hat; St Gregory the Great with dove and Papal tiara; St Augustine of Hippo with flaming heart and crozier; St Remigius of Rheims; on north side of buttress is St John the Evangelist; then, in a line above the three central doors: on the buttress the Virgin Mary with dove upon her shoulder (emblem of the Holy Spirit); St Barbara with tower, book and palm; St Catherine with wheel and sword; St Roche with dog and plague-spot; St Nicholas of Myra ('Santa Claus') with staff and three golden balls; St George, Patron Saint of England, trampling on a dragon; St Christopher with the Christ-Child on his shoulder; St Sebastian with arrows; St Cosmas with

ointment box; St Damian with pestle and mortar; St Margaret of Antioch with dragon, cross and palm; St Ursula with arrow and palm; on the buttress is St John the Baptist; and on the buttress on the right are St Stephen holding stones; St Lucy with lamp and dagger; St Agatha with pincers (her breasts were torn from her body with pincers); St Agnes with lamb; and St Cecilia, Patron Saint of music with organ.

5th Tier   *The bottom level, most easily seen.*
Contains 14 bishops, founders, martyrs, princes & other worthies.
Round the corner on the north side of the cathedral are, from left to right: St Birinus, the first Bishop in Wessex, who settled at Dorchester, Oxfordshire (note the fish on his pediment); St Etheldreda, Founder of Ely Abbey (where Ely Cathedral now stands) holding a model of a church; King Henry VI, who founded Eton College and King's College Cambridge. Then on the West Front are: a Bishop, possibly Giles de Bridport in whose time Salisbury Cathedral was consecrated in 1258; Bishop Richard Poore, founder of the Cathedral, holding a model of a church; Henry III, a generous benefactor while the cathedral was being built and who attended its consecration; St Edmund of Canterbury, former Treasurer of Salisbury Cathedral and later Archbishop of Canterbury; Bishop Odo of Ramsbury with chalice; on the north side of buttress is Bishop Ken of Bath and Wells (1637–1711), the hymn-writer (this statue was added in 1931); on the buttress is St Osmund, Patron Saint of Salisbury (see pages 38–9); above the smaller left arch is the Angel Gabriel; above the central arch is the Virgin Mary with lily; above the right arch is the Virgin of the Annunciation. Immediately over the main door is the Virgin holding Jesus in her arms; and on either side is a censing angel. Then, on the buttress is Bishop Brithwold of Ramsbury; on the south side of the buttress is a new statue of George Herbert (1593–1633, poet and Rector of Bemerton (see pages 92–3); on the far buttress are St Alban with sceptre; St Alphege holding bones (he was pelted to death with stones and ox bones by the Danes), St Edmund, King and Martyr (murdered by the Danes) with dagger; and St Thomas Becket with cross staff and with dagger in his head, reminding us of his murder in Canterbury Cathedral.

As well as all these statues there are also a number of gargoyles and curious heads of demons.

Above: Line of statues above the three central doors on the West Front:
Virgin Mary with dove,
St Barbara with tower book and palm,
St Catherine with wheel and sword,
St Roche with dog and plague-spot,
St Nicholas with three golden balls,
St George with dragon,
St Christopher with Christchild on shoulder,
St Sebastian with arrows,
St Cosmas with ointment-box,
St Damian with pestle and mortar,
St Margaret with dragon cross and palm,
St Ursula with arrow and palm.

Below, left: St Alphege with stones (he was pelted to death by the Danes).

Below, centre: The new statue of George Herbert, carved by Jason Battle and placed in position on the West Front in 2003.

Below, right: St Edmund King and Martyr with dagger (he was killed by the Vikings).

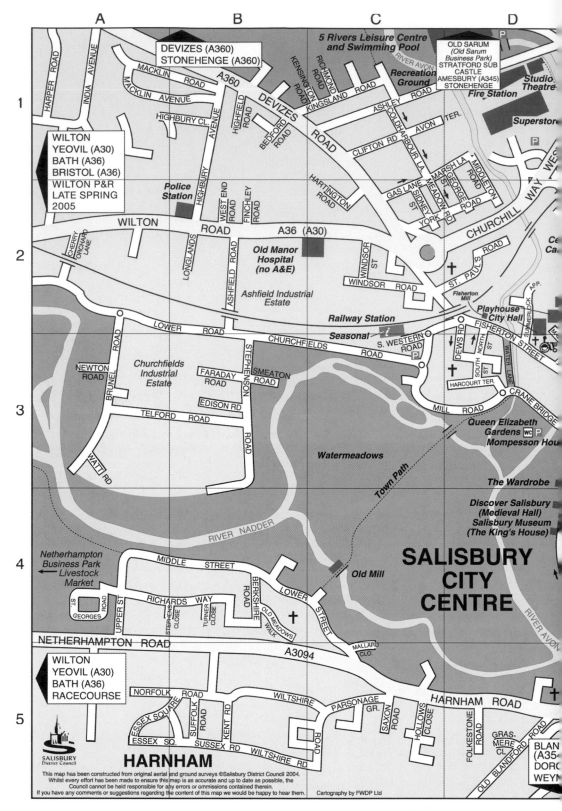

Map of present-day Salisbury.

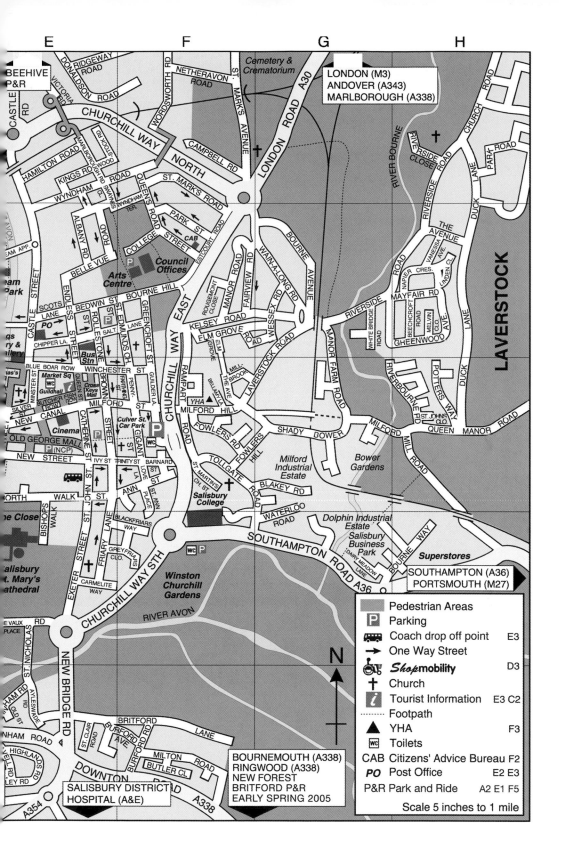

FIVE FACTS ABOUT THE
PRISONERS OF CONSCIENCE WINDOW

If we look towards the high altar, our eyes are immediately attracted by the blaze of stained glass, predominantly blue, filling the five tall lancet windows at the far eastern end of the Trinity Chapel. Together they form the *Prisoners of Conscience* window, and were specially commissioned in 1979 to enrich this part of the cathedral with meaning and beauty.

1.   *It was designed and made in France by Gabriel Loire and Jacques Loire.* Gabriel Loire, assisted by his son Jacques, created these windows in his workshop in the village of Lèves, just outside Chartres in France. Gabriel Loire had lived and worked near Chartres all his life, and the stained glass he produced for Salisbury Cathedral is directly inspired by the windows of Chartres Cathedral.

2.   *It was unveiled in 1980 by Yehudi Menuhin.* Having been commissioned in March 1979, the five panels were received exactly one year later, in March 1980, and the unveiling ceremony took place two months later, on 14 May. The windows were unveiled by the great Jewish musician Yehudi Menuhin, and dedicated by George Reindorp, Bishop of Salisbury.

3.   *The two outer windows show prisoners of conscience in the twentieth century.* Each of the shorter windows is divided into twelve panels. The outer windows show myriads of faces of people who have stood up for justice and truth against the forces of oppression.

4.   *The three central windows show Jesus as a prisoner of conscience in the first century.* The central window is divided into twenty-four panels. The shower of gold at the top symbolises God's acceptance of Jesus' stand for truth. Jesus' head, as He hangs on the cross, is seen at the apex of a triangle of light. This triangle of light shines upon the graves of prisoners of conscience within an orb representing the world of humanity.

      In the lower half the ascending spiral expresses the theme of resurrection, of life through death, and of the stand of Jesus against his oppressors.

      In the left-hand lancet of the central three, Jesus is shown standing before Pontius Pilate – it is the authority of God encountering the tyranny of men; truth versus lies.

      In the right-hand lancet of the central three, Jesus stands dressed up by the mocking soldiers with the crown of thorns and the purple robe.

      In the central lancet, Jesus is shown crucified, with the figure of the mother standing at the foot of the cross.

5.   *The essential meaning of the windows.* Sydney H. Evans, former Dean of Salisbury, whose vision it was to commission this work of modern Christian art, has summed up its meaning in these words:

'Evil turned into goodness by love, falsehood overcome by suffering allegiance to truth; these are the fundamental affirmations of the window, to be seen in the upward flowing movements of design and colour to be met with the descending movement of the glory in gold. The great affirmation of Christian faith in the transfiguring power of the risen Christ in the history of humanity is given new and contemporary expression in this great work of art.'

Detail from the *Prisoners of Conscience* window.

A man that looks on glass
  On it may stay his eye;
Or if he pleaseth, through it pass,
  And then the heaven espy.

(George Herbert, 1593–1633)

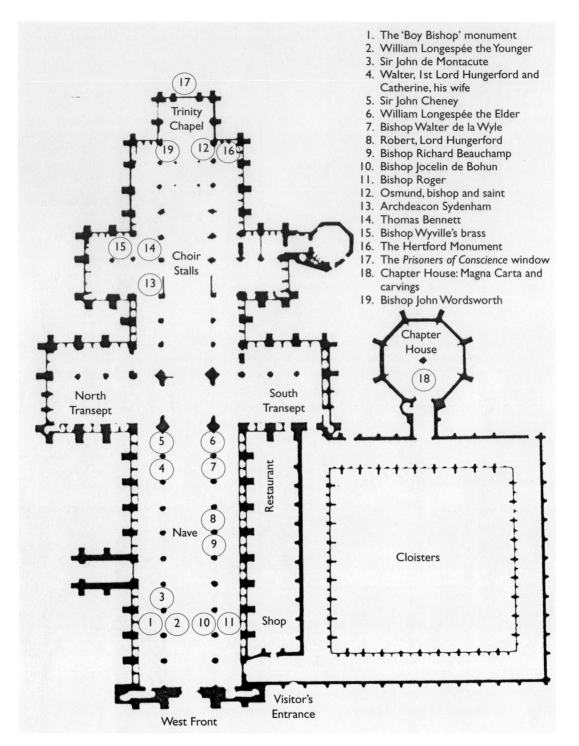

1. The 'Boy Bishop' monument
2. William Longespée the Younger
3. Sir John de Montacute
4. Walter, 1st Lord Hungerford and Catherine, his wife
5. Sir John Cheney
6. William Longespée the Elder
7. Bishop Walter de la Wyle
8. Robert, Lord Hungerford
9. Bishop Richard Beauchamp
10. Bishop Jocelin de Bohun
11. Bishop Roger
12. Osmund, bishop and saint
13. Archdeacon Sydenham
14. Thomas Bennett
15. Bishop Wyville's brass
16. The Hertford Monument
17. The *Prisoners of Conscience* window
18. Chapter House: Magna Carta and carvings
19. Bishop John Wordsworth

Trinity Chapel

Choir Stalls

North Transept

South Transept

Chapter House

Restaurant

Nave

Cloisters

Shop

West Front

Visitor's Entrance

Ground plan of Salisbury Cathedral showing some of the principal monuments and items of interest.

TWELVE STORIES ABOUT THE EFFIGY MEMORIALS IN THE NAVE

PART ONE: NORTH SIDE

This tour of the memorials in the nave starts on the north side, opposite the Old Clock. The memorials are described here in the order found as you move towards the east end of the cathedral.

1. *The 'Boy Bishop' – who swaps places with the real Bishop of Salisbury*

Opposite the Old Clock at the west end of the north aisle there is a tiny effigy of a bishop. No one knows the exact history of this little monument, but one story is told that it represents a 'Boy Bishop', who may have died during his brief period of office.

In the Middle Ages there was a curious custom in the weeks leading up to Christmas, when bishop and clergy swapped places with the choirboys! The boys sat in places normally occupied by the priests and conducted the services (except for Mass), while the clergy acted as their humble attendants. For a few weeks, the head chorister became, in effect, the Bishop of Salisbury. This medieval custom was widespread throughout Europe, and lasted for several centuries – possibly a relic of the old Roman festivities of the 'Feast of Fools', when servants and masters changed places.

It has been conjectured that such a 'Boy Bishop' is remembered by the little tomb. However, this is probably a fanciful guess. More likely it was carved to mark the spot where a bishop's heart was buried. Whatever the truth, it is an odd little memorial.

In recent years the old custom has been revived in a ceremony taking place around the time of the Feast of the Holy Innocents (6 December). The Bishop of Salisbury hands his staff to a chorister and installs him on his throne. The boy preaches a sermon (which he writes himself) and blesses the people. It is an annual ceremony that is a lesson in humility and a recognition of the wisdom of youthful innocence.

Top: Small memorial of the 'Boy Bishop' on the south side of the nave.

Right: Modern photograph of 'Boy Bishop'.

William Longespée the Younger – no 'long-tailed coward'

There are *two* William Longespées buried in Salisbury Cathedral: father and son. This one, whose memorial is on the north side, is the son, who died with spectacular bravery in 1250 at the battle of Mansourah in Egypt, during one of the crusades.

In 1249 William Longespée the Younger led 200 English knights to join Louis IX of France (Saint Louis) in fighting the Saracen forces. Although they were supposed to be allies, the French and the English were often quarrelling among themselves, and the French nobles taunted the English for being 'long-tailed cowards'. This was just before the battle of Mansourah, and Longespée replied: 'I shall go today where you will not dare to keep level with the tail of my horse!'

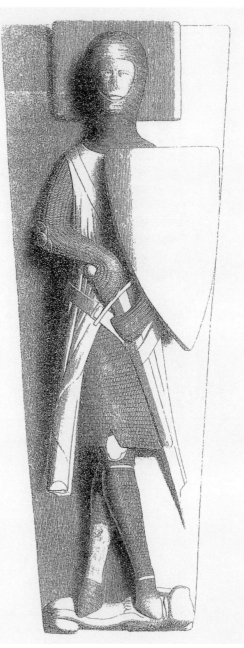

True to his word, Longespée dashed into the thick of the fighting in a suicidal display of daredevilry. The Saracen forces won; Longespée was killed; and the French King Louis was captured.

Even the Saracen leader was impressed, and had Longespée's body buried with honour. Later, Christians reburied him at the Church of the Holy Cross at Acre. Longespée became regarded as a martyr in England. This monument in Salisbury Cathedral probably marks an empty tomb. In fact, Salisbury Cathedral was still being built when Longespée was killed.

William Longespée the Younger, killed in battle in 1250 – no 'long-tailed coward'.

3   *Sir John de Montacute, 'King of the Isle of Man'*

This knight died in 1390, during the reign of Richard II, at the period when Chaucer was writing his *Canterbury Tales*. It is likely that Sir John and Geoffrey Chaucer met one another at court. As a young man, Sir John had fought with the Black Prince at the Battle of Crécy in 1346, in the reign of Edward III.

Sir John de Montacute must have been a trusted man of affairs at court, for he was given the responsibility of escorting the fifteen-year-old Anne of Bohemia across the Channel to London in 1382, to become the queen of Richard II.

Impressively, he was referred to as 'King of the Isle of Man' – and the arms of the Isle of Man are on his tomb. At this time, the title of 'King of the Isle of Man' was customarily given to a favourite noble by the King of England. Such a title would explain the crown at his head and the lion at his feet. His elaborate armour is a sign of wealth and importance. For an explanation of the rebus on his coat of arms (found on the ends of this memorial) see page 41.

In his will Sir John asked to be buried in St Paul's Cathedral if he died in London, but that if he died elsewhere, his body should lie in Salisbury Cathedral.

4.   *Walter, Lord Hungerford, Knight of the Garter, and Catherine his wife*

The double tomb of the Hungerfords is one of the few tombs that are in their original position. There are several Hungerfords buried in the cathedral. This one, Sir Walter, died in 1449, just before the Wars of the Roses.

5.   *Sir John Cheney, a seven-foot giant and Standard Bearer of Henry VII*

When this alabaster tomb was opened, it was found that Sir John Cheney had been about 7ft tall – a massive giant of a man, who must have been a fearsome warrior as he fought for Henry Tudor, helping him to beat Richard III at the Battle of Bosworth Field.

Cheney was in the thick of the fighting, next to Henry Tudor himself, and heroically clashed steel against steel with King Richard III (the 'hunchback'). Giant though he was, Cheney fell off his horse under King Richard's blows, and it was left to others to overcome Richard.

He fought valiantly, helping greatly to secure victory for the Tudors. Therefore, after his coronation Henry rewarded Cheney by making him Knight of the Garter, Privy Councillor, and a Baron. Cheney died in 1509, in the first year of Henry VIII's reign.

If you cross over from Sir John Cheney's tomb to the other side of the nave, the tomb nearest the transept is that of William Longespée the Elder, who was the first person to be buried in the cathedral. Start at this tomb and then go back to the west end.

6. *William Longespée the Elder — and a poisoned rat*

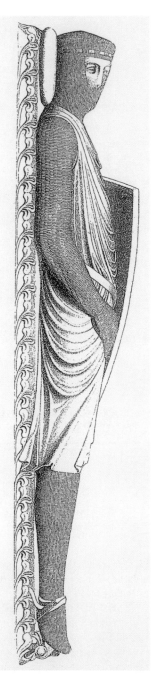

This is one of the most interesting memorials in the cathedral, marking the tomb of a bastard son of Henry II — William Longespée, Earl of Salisbury and half-brother of two kings of England, Richard I ('Lionheart'), and King John.

He had been 'given' the twelve-year-old Ela, Countess of Salisbury, as his bride, and thereby he acquired the Earldom of Salisbury. Because of this, it was only natural that he and Ela should each lay a foundation stone of Salisbury's new cathedral at the foundation ceremony in 1220. It was only natural, too, that at his death, almost six years later, in 1226, he should become the first person to be buried here.

The six lions on his shield proclaim his royal parentage, and in his eventful life he gained a great naval victory against the French; beseiged Ghent; fought against Welsh rebels; led an army in support of Henry III at the battle of Lincoln; and defended Guienne against King Louis of France in 1225. Perhaps his most important act was to counsel his half-brother King John to yield to the demands of the barons, and he was present at Runnymede when John put his seal to Magna Carta.

Such a busy life inevitably led to his being away from home for long periods of time, and his young wife Ela must have felt somewhat neglected. Small wonder that when Longespée was reported drowned she prepared to marry someone else. Just imagine her feelings when her husband turned up back at Salisbury, still alive and well.

There was a great feast to celebrate his home-coming. Then, dramatically, Longespée suddenly died. Was he poisoned? And if so, by whom?

Centuries later, when his tomb was opened, a dead rat carrying traces of arsenic was found inside his skull. People still wonder . . .

Monumental effigy of William Longespée the Elder (d. 1226), half-brother of King Richard I and King John.

7.   *Walter de la Wyle, Bishop of Salisbury 1263–71*

Bishop de la Wyle's tomb comes next as you walk towards the west end. He was the fifth bishop of the new cathedral, so he was among the first to enjoy the completed building – though the spire was yet to be added. Wyle founded the College and Church of St Edmund in Salisbury, as a memorial to Edmund Rich, Canon and Treasurer of the cathedral as it was being built.

8.   *Robert, Lord Hungerford, d. 1459*

This impressive memorial marks the resting place of Robert, Lord Hungerford, who fought in the French wars in the time of Henry V and Henry VI. This superb effigy displays the typical armour of the fifteenth century. Notice his short hair, fashionable at the time, and the ruff, or 'SS collar', which he wears as a Lancastrian badge. There are pieces of the old Hungerford Chapel, originally built to honour Robert, but destroyed by James Wyatt in the 1790s, incorporated into this monument.

9.   *Bishop Richard Beauchamp, 1450–81*

Bishop Beauchamp should be remembered in gratitude for having erected the strainer arches across the entrances to the north and south transepts, in order to strengthen the supports of the tower. Arguably, if he had not undertaken this work, the spire would have collapsed centuries ago.

10.   *Bishop Jocelin de Bohun, 1142–84*

11.   *Bishop Roger, 1107–39*

Both these memorial slabs came from the first cathedral, built at Old Sarum. Bishop Roger was Salisbury's third bishop, and Bishop Jocelin was the fourth. Jocelin was one of the bishops excommunicated by Thomas Becket for taking part in the coronation of Henry 'The Young King'. This excommunication was the final straw for King Henry II, and led to his angry outburst 'Who will rid me of this turbulent priest?' Becket was murdered in Canterbury Cathedral, and, following this, Bishop Jocelin resigned and retired to a monastery.

Memorial slab of Bishop Jocelin de Bohun (1142–70) – one of three bishops whose remains were brought down from Old Sarum to the new cathedral on 14 June 1226.
    Thomas Becket was so furious with Jocelin for taking part in the coronation of Henry 'the Young King' (Henry II's son) that he excommunicated him in 1170. The sequence of events that followed this excommunication led to Becket's murder in Canterbury Cathedral. Jocelin retired to a monastery, dying in 1184.

THE STORY OF THE HERTFORD MONUMENT

A ROYAL COUPLE WHO ENRAGED QUEEN ELIZABETH I

At the end of the south choir aisle is an elaborate Elizabethan tomb with beautifully-carved effigies of the Earl and Countess of Hertford.

Their love affair created scandal, for they actually dared to marry in secret without telling the queen – Elizabeth I.

The fact is, they were both related to the Queen, for the Earl was a member of the Seymour family, and his lover, Katherine, was a younger sister of Lady Jane Grey, the 'nine days' queen', who had been beheaded for allowing herself to be drawn into the plot to usurp the throne when Edward VI had died. Katherine Grey herself was spoken of as a successor to the throne, should Elizabeth die childless.

Anyone related to the queen was required by law to gain her consent to marry. Nevertheless, Edward Seymour and the twenty-year-old Katherine Grey went ahead secretly with their marriage. It was several months before the Queen discovered their guilty secret, and when she learned of their marriage she flung them both as prisoners in the Tower of London.

In theory, they should have been kept apart, but helpful gaolers allowed them to see each other – and in the course of time Katherine had a baby boy. Even worse, after the elapse of more time, she produced another.

The Queen was so livid with rage that she ordered that the couple should never meet again. And they never did. They were immediately taken from the Tower and kept under house arrest in separate country houses. Poor Katherine never regained freedom, and never saw her husband again. She died four years later, in 1568, still in disgrace, having sent a deathbed letter to the Queen, begging her to be kind to the Earl and her two sons.

Queen Elizabeth must have had a twinge of conscience, for she paid for Katherine to be given a ceremonial funeral in Salisbury Cathedral, and she pardoned the Earl of Hertford, eventually releasing him after eight years of imprisonment.

He married again – twice – but at his death he asked that he should be buried beside Katherine – the wife that he had never been allowed to live with.

Also shown in this elaborate memorial are their two sons – born in the Tower of London. They are depicted kneeling on each side, below their parents. As boys, they were cared for by William Cecil, Lord Burghley, who brought them up with his own children.

The Hertford Monument. (See the story behind this memorial on the opposite page.)

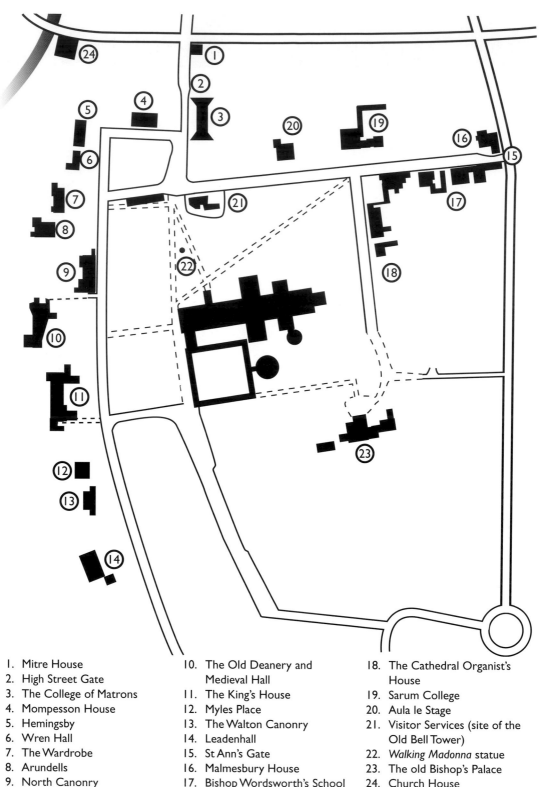

1. Mitre House
2. High Street Gate
3. The College of Matrons
4. Mompesson House
5. Hemingsby
6. Wren Hall
7. The Wardrobe
8. Arundells
9. North Canonry
10. The Old Deanery and Medieval Hall
11. The King's House
12. Myles Place
13. The Walton Canonry
14. Leadenhall
15. St Ann's Gate
16. Malmesbury House
17. Bishop Wordsworth's School
18. The Cathedral Organist's House
19. Sarum College
20. Aula le Stage
21. Visitor Services (site of the Old Bell Tower)
22. *Walking Madonna* statue
23. The old Bishop's Palace
24. Church House

Map of the Close, showing some of the most important houses.

PART THREE

The City of Salisbury and its People

SEVEN FACTS FOR STARTERS

Salisbury is unique in many respects. Perhaps the essential fact to remember is that the city and cathedral were planned by its medieval bishop as a completely new town in 1220. The layout of the centre of the city is still exactly as it was originally planned. We have already looked at the cathedral and the Close, which is virtually a separate 'village'. Here are some basic facts about the present-day City of New Sarum.

1.   *It is a city.* In Britain, the term 'city' does not automatically apply to all towns, neither does it apply only to towns that have cathedrals. British towns are granted the special status of being a 'city' by virtue of having been granted a Royal Charter. When Salisbury was founded in 1220, it 'belonged' to the bishop. It did not achieve full independence from the bishop until James I granted it a charter in 1612.

2.   *The population of Salisbury at the turn of this century was 39,530.* This is surprisingly small for a modern city, and it means that there are no large sprawling suburbs. It has no heavy industry. Most of its wealth in the past came from the wool trade, when Salisbury Plain supported hundreds of thousands of sheep. Much of its wealth nowadays comes from its tourist industry.

3.   *The city and cathedral attract over four million day visitors every year.*

4.   *Markets are held on Tuesdays and Saturdays.* A charter of 1227 granted New Sarum the right to hold a weekly market on Tuesdays, and in 1315 a second weekly market was allowed to take place on Saturdays. Both markets are still held today. If you can, visit Salisbury on a market day.

5.   *Salisbury escaped bombing in the Second World War.* A few bombs were dropped on the outskirts of the city, but the centre of the city was left intact. Because there was no need for major rebuilding, no modern high-rise office blocks or flats intrude on the skyline. No tall buildings are allowed. The planners of 1220 would still easily find their way around the main part of the city.

6.   *There are 57 places of worship in the city apart from the Cathedral.*

7.   *And there are 123 pubs,* some of which date from the time when workmen building the new cathedral in the thirteenth century needed to quench their thirsts (see pages 82–7).

NINE OLDER NAMES OF SALISBURY

1. *Sorviodunum or Sorbiodunum.* The name used by the Romans, noting that it was nineteen miles from Venta Belgarum (Winchester) on the way to Isca Dumnoniorum (Exeter). It is possible that 'Sorviodunum' was a Latinised version of a Celtic phrase meaning 'fort by the slow-flowing river'. 'Dunon' was a British word referring to hill forts.

2. *Searobyrg.* The Saxon name as used in the *Anglo-Saxon Chronicle.* This may have been associated with the Old English word *Searu*, meaning 'armour', and another Old English word *Burg*, meaning 'town' was added to this. Later, the first 'r' was exchanged for 'l', in Norman pronunciation.

3. *Serebrig.* Another version of 'Searobyrg'. This spelling is found on a gold coin minted at Old Sarum in the reign of King Ethelred the Unready (978–1016).

4. *Sarisberie.* This was the name given to Old Sarum in the Domesday Book of 1086.

5. *Sarum.* Used in 1091. (Anyone puzzled by the limerick on the next page should try substituting 'Sarum' for 'Salisbury'.)

6. *Vetus Sarum.* 'Old Sarum', used in 1195.

7. *Salesbir.* Used in 1206.

8. *Nova Sarisberia.* Used in 1227, following the establishment of the new cathedral site in 1220, with houses being built around it.

9. *Salisburia.* This, with several variations, eventually gave us the present name. It may have been adapted to resemble the name of Salzburg, or 'city of salt' – though there is no connection with that city.

FIVE RHYMES ABOUT SALISBURY

1.

No better place in England is
For wholesome ayre and water pure
And all that maketh life endure
Than that fayre city, Sarum hight*
Whereof my book I now endite.

(Anon.)

(* 'which is called Sarum')

2.

[Salisbury is famous for]
The height of its steeple,
The pride of its people,
Its scissors and knives,*
And diligent wives.

(Old saying)

(* Salisbury was formerly a famous cutlery-making centre)

3.

Query 'tis 'twixt folk and steeple
Which is most lofty, Spire or People?

(Old saying)

4.

Had Adam come here, sent from Paradise,
His place of exile would have seemed more fine;
Nuts weigh down the trees, scents assail the air,
Birds sport in song, and earth bursts rich with flowers.

(Henry d'Avranches, thirteenth-century poet)

5.

There was a young curate of Salisbury
Whose manners were quite halisbury-scalisbury;
    He ran about Hampshire
    Without any pampshire,
Till his bishop compelled him to walisbury.

(Anon.)

FIVE STRIPES ON THE COAT OF ARMS

Salisbury's coat of arms (shown on p. 68) shows five horizontal bands or stripes, which represent the five rivers that meet in the water meadows. The Wiltshire River Avon is augmented by four other rivers here. It then turns south to flow into the sea at Christchurch in Dorset. In the seventeenth and eighteenth centuries a grand scheme was begun to make the Avon fully navigable, so that ships could sail directly from London to Salisbury, but after several attempts to make the scheme work, it was eventually abandoned. If it had succeeded, Salisbury might well have become an important inland port. These are Salisbury's five rivers.

1.   *Avon* is a name dating from the time of the ancient Britons. Throughout the British Isles there are many 'Avon' names. It simply means a river.

2.   *Bourne*, deriving from the Old English word *burna*, means a stream.

3.   *Ebble*, an obscure word, probably dialect, means aspen tree or white poplar. These trees probably grew along its banks.

4.   *Nadder* derives from a name used by the ancient Britons, meaning to flow.

5.   *Wylye*, another ancient British derivation, comes from a word meaning 'to trick'. The name means 'tricky river' – that is, one that is liable to produce floods when it overflows its banks.

ARMS OF THE TOWN AND BOROUGH OF NEW SARUM

The correct heraldic description of Salisbury's coat of arms (see p. 68) is officially described by William Harvey, Clarenceux King of Arms, in his Visitation of Wiltshire, 1565.

Arms: *Barry of eight Azure and Or* (i.e. there are eight bars or stripes, blue and gold).

Supporters: *Two eagles displayed Or, ducally crowned, beaked and legged Azure* (i.e. these golden eagles are wearing duke's crowns, and having blue beaks and legs).

William Harvey comments: 'These Arms, w'th the two Egles supporting the same, are the Auntient Armes belonging and Appertaining to the Maior, his bretheren, and comonalities of New Sarum, the w'ch I have regesterd and recorded in the Regester of my Visitation now made within the Com. of Wilts . . .'.

TWENTY SQUARES OR 'CHEQUERS'

When Bishop Richard Poore designed his new cathedral, he also designed a new city to grow up with it. Basically, the layout of the streets in the centre of modern Salisbury is exactly the same as Richard Poore's original plan.

He designed his new city in the form of a rectangular grid, with five parallel streets running north to south, and six parallel streets running east to west. The squares thus formed were called 'chequers' and over the years these became named after a pub or some well-known citizen.

There are still tell-tale names left to remind us of those early years. Here are the names of the chequers as they appear in the map of Salisbury overleaf. This map was published in 1751, but the chequers are still the same today.

1.	White Horse Chequer
2.	Gores Chequer
3.	Parsons Chequer
4.	Vanners Chequer
5.	Blew Bore Chequer (Blue Boar Row still exists)
6.	Swans Chequer
7.	3 Cups Chequer
8.	Griffin Chequer
9.	Mitre Chequer
10.	Cross Keys Chequer
11.	Black Horse Chequer
12.	Swayns Chequer (Swayne was a rich wool merchant)
13.	New Street Chequer (New Street, which still exists, was probably the first street to be built)
14.	Antelope Chequer
15.	Trinity Chequer
16.	Rolfes Chequer
17.	Bernards-cross Chequer
18.	White Hart Chequer (the White Hart is still one of Salisbury's foremost inns, see page 87)
19.	Marsh Chequer
20.	Pound Chequer

The streets that surround this pattern of chequers are (clockwise): on the northern boundary, Scots Lane and Bedwin Street; on the eastern boundary, Greencroft Street, Guilder Lane, Culver Street, and Dolphin Street; on the southern boundary, St Ann Street, St John Street, and New Street; on the western boundary, High Street, Silver Street, Minster Street, and Castle Street.

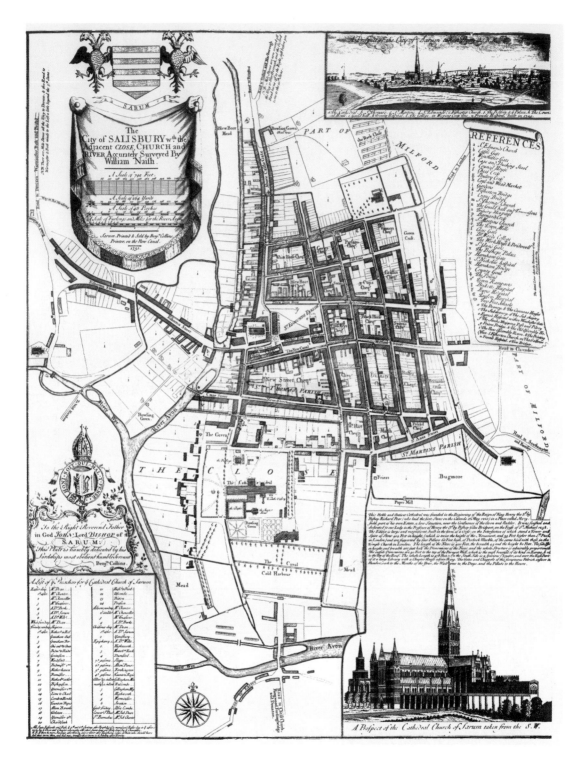

Map of Salisbury 'printed and sold by Benjamin Collins on the New Canal, 1751', and detail (opposite) showing the old 'chequers' and the system of canals running through many of the streets. (Compare this map with that of the modern city given on pages 54–5.)

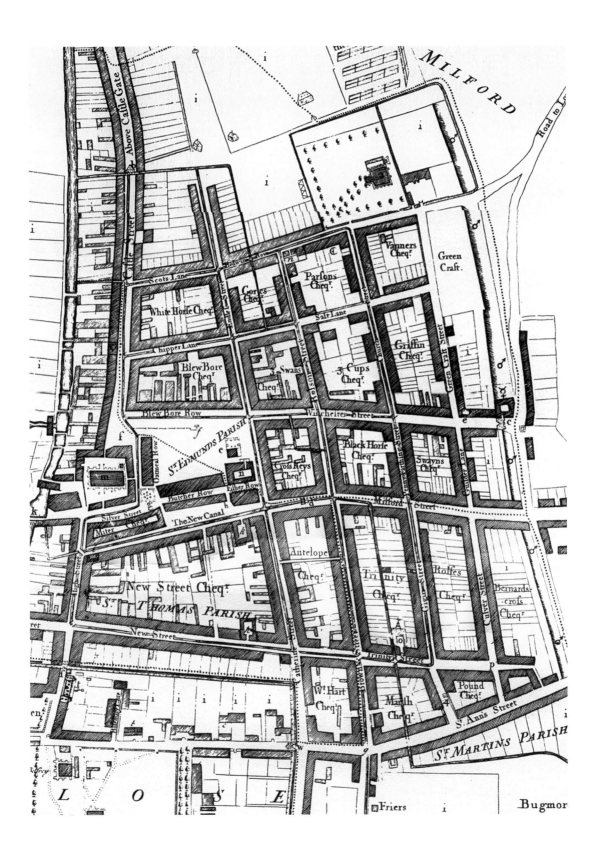

TWENTY-THREE STREETS THROUGH WHICH THE OLD CANALS USED TO FLOW

For more than six hundred years, canals and open conduits ran through many of the streets in the centre of Salisbury. They were a notable feature of the city until well into the nineteenth century.

There were two canal systems, both leading out of the River Avon, and the canals ran in an elaborate pattern not only through the streets but also through the middle of some of the 'chequers' (see map on page 73).

In earlier centuries there were many little bridges over these canals, but these had to be demolished as traffic increased and more wagons trundled through the streets.

Rather fancifully, Salisbury gained the reputation of being the 'English Venice', but in reality these canals were little more than smelly open sewers, and became a dangerous health hazard in Victorian times.

It was not until 1875 that the last 'canal' was filled in. Its name today – New Canal – is the only reminder of its watery past.

The map of 1751, on page 72, shows just how extensive this network was, flowing through twenty-three streets.

1.	Bedwin Street
2.	Blue Boar Row
3.	Brown Street
4.	Castle Street
5.	Catherine Street
6.	Chipper Lane
7.	Endless Street
8.	Exeter Street (which was formerly called Draghall Street)
9.	Gigant Street
10.	High Street
11.	Ivy Street
12.	Milford Street
13.	Minster Street
14.	New Street
15.	New Canal
16.	Pennyfarthing Street
17.	Rollestone Street
18.	St Edmund's Street
19.	Salt Lane
20.	Scots Lane
21.	Silver Street
22.	Trinity Street
23.	Winchester Street

When these canals were filled in, hundreds of objects were found, which had been lost or thrown into them. A collection of keys, combs, scissors, knives, coins, etc., are on display in Salisbury Museum (see page 100).

Minster Street in the late eighteenth century, showing the state of the canals.

THREE DESCRIPTIONS OF THE STREET CANALS

The streets through which the old canals used to flow are the subject of many picturesque paintings, many of which can be seen in Salisbury Museum. Some well-known writers also described them – sometimes in scathing terms.

1. 'There be many fair streates in the City of Saresbyri, and especially the High Streate and the Castel Streate, so called because it lyith as a way to the Castelle of Old Saresbyri. All the Streates, in a manner, of New Saresbyri hath little streamelettes and arms derived out of Avon that renneth through them. The site of the very toun of Saresbyri and much ground thereabout is playne and low, and as a pan or receiver of most part of the water of Wyleshire.'

(John Leland (1506–52, a prebend of Salisbury and 'King's Antiquary' to Henry VIII, in his book *The Itinerary*)

2. 'In the city of Salisbury doe reigne the dropsy, consumption, scurvy, gowte; it is an exceeding dampish place.'

(John Aubrey (1626–97), *The Natural History of Wiltshire*, first pub. 1847)

3. 'Salisbury itself is indeed a large and pleasant city; tho' I do not think it at all the pleasanter for that which they boast so much of; namely, the water running thro' the middle of every street, or that it adds any thing to the beauty of the place, but just the contrary; it keeps the streets always dirty, full of wet and filth, and weeds, even in the middle of summer.'

(Daniel Defoe (1660–1731), *A Tour through the Whole Island of Great Britain*, first published 1724–6)

A WELSH HARPIST SOOTHES HENRY V'S BRAWLING TROOPS

In 1415, before the battle of Agincourt, as Henry V was preparing to invade France, some of his soldiers were billeted in Fisherton (near Salisbury's present-day railway station). One night, Salisbury apprentices started brawling with these soldiers on Fisherton bridge, and soon the city was threatened with a tremendous fight.

Luckily, a Welsh minstrel happened to be passing. He leaped up on the wall of the bridge and began playing his harp. One by one the men beneath him stopped fighting and turned to listen to his wonderful music. The city was saved from vandalism.

Salisbury city records mention the reward given 'to a certain minstrel of Wales for purchasing peace, and for making him a hood, because he lost his hood in defence of the city, in the insult offered on the bridge at Fisherton by the men of the Earl of Lancaster'.

NINE TRADENAMES OF STREETS AND PLACES

The street names of Salisbury provide an interesting link with its past. It is worth looking at the names of the streets, particularly near the Poultry Cross. Here are nine names associated with various trades.

1.	Butcher Row	6.	Pennyfarthing Street
2.	Fish Row	7.	Poultry Cross
3.	Mill Stream Approach	8.	Salt Lane
4.	Oatmeal Row	9.	Silver Street
5.	Ox Row		

Pennyfarthing Street gained its name in the thirteenth century, when it was the area where workmen camped as they built the cathedral. The men felt that they were not being paid properly, so they went on strike.

They were earning just one penny a day – but they demanded an extra farthing. In other words they wanted a 25 per cent rise!

Street names showing trades and perhaps an old profession.

77

Every Tuesday and Saturday for almost 700 years the Poultry Cross has been the site of market stall-holders. This twenty-first-century scene is typical.

THE LEGEND OF THE POULTRY CROSS

The Poultry Cross, standing at the end of Butcher Row, is one of the favourite familiar sights of Salisbury, still used by stallholders on market days to shelter their goods from the effects of the weather.

There is a story about the origin of this Poultry Cross – that a fourteenth-century knight, Laurence de St Martin, received the sacrament one Easter, and, instead of eating it on the spot, galloped home and ate some with oysters, some with onions, and the rest with wine.

Such a sacriligious act demanded severe punishment, so the Bishop commanded him to erect a stone cross on which the whole history of the affair was to be inscribed. The naughty knight was to go there, barefoot and bareheaded and dressed only in his shirt every Friday for the rest of his life, and do penance for his sin.

In fact, the Poultry Cross was first mentioned in 1335 as being the site of the poultry and vegetable market. It was modernised in 1711, and in 1853 it was given its present 'medieval' roof.

THREE MORE LOST MARKET CROSSES

In the Middle Ages Salisbury had no fewer than four market crosses, of which the Poultry Cross is the only one to survive. The other three crosses were: the *Cheese Cross*, situated at the south end of Castle Street, in the triangle near the entrance to the City Library (this area is still called the Cheese Market); the *Wool Cross*, situated in what is now the New Canal; and *Barnewell's Cross*, situated in St Barnard's Street, where the cattle market was held.

The Poultry Cross.

TWENTY-SIX ROYAL VISITORS

Most English kings and queens have visited Salisbury at one time or other, for various reasons. Here are some of the more memorable.

1 & 2.	*Henry III* came to oversee the construction of the cathedral while it was being built, and was present, with his queen, *Eleanor of Provence*, at its consecration on 30 September 1258.
3.	*Edward I* held his Parliament in Salisbury in March 1297.
4.	*Edward III* visited the cathedral on 1 September 1340. After this visit he gave permission for the Close wall to be built, using stone from the old cathedral at Old Sarum.
5 & 6.	*Edward 'the Black Prince'*, son of Edward III, visited Salisbury in May 1357, with his captive, *King John of France*.
7.	*Richard II* was furious with his Parliament here in April 1384, accusing his uncle, John of Gaunt, of treachery.
8.	*Henry VI* sat with judges in Salisbury in July 1451, trying the followers of the rebel leader, Jack Cade. Later, a quarter-piece of Jack Cade's body was sent to Salisbury to be publicly exhibited as a warning to would-be traitors. Cade's followers had murdered the bishop of Salisbury (see page 21). Henry VI was a frequent visitor to Salisbury.
9.	*Richard III* came with armed forces to Salisbury in November 1483, at the time of the Duke of Buckingham's rebellion. The Duke was beheaded in Salisbury marketplace (see page 98).
10 & 11.	*Henry VII* visited Salisbury in 1488, 1491 and 1496. On this last visit he was accompanied by his queen, *Elizabeth of York*.
12, 13 & 14.	*Henry VIII* came in 1511, again in 1514 with his first Queen, *Catherine of Aragon*, and then again in 1535, together with his second queen, *Anne Boleyn*, who was presented with a purse containing 28 marks (£20 15½p). On this occasion Henry and Anne probably stayed at what is now Church House in Crane Street.
15.	*James I* greatly enjoyed visiting Salisbury and often came here during his reign. At first he used to stay at the Bishop's Palace, but later he would stay at what became known as 'the King's House' in the Close. This now houses the Salisbury and South Wiltshire Museum. Importantly, James granted Salisbury its Charter in 1612, so giving the city independence from the power of the bishop.

16 & 17.	*Charles II* spent much of August 1665 in Salisbury, with his queen, *Catherine of Braganza*, trying to escape the Great Plague of London. Nell Gwynne, though not a 'royal', was one of Charles's favourite mistresses. She also came to Salisbury at this time, and bought a pair of Salisbury-made scissors for the extraordinary sum of one hundred guineas.

18.	*James II* came here in November 1688, to take command of his army to fight the invading forces of William of Orange. James suffered an appalling nose-bleed while he was in Salisbury. This affected him so badly that John Churchill (the future Duke of Marlborough) deserted from James's army and went over to join William of Orange. James, with his nose still bleeding, returned to London and prepared to flee the country.

19.	*William III* (William of Orange) stayed at the Bishop's Palace on 4 December 1688, on his way from Brixham to London, where he was to be crowned as William III, replacing James II as king.

20 & 21.	*George III*, who 'discovered' Weymouth as his favourite holiday resort, frequently came to Salisbury with his queen, *Charlotte*. During one of his visits, he asked if he might provide a new organ for the cathedral, 'from a gentleman of Berkshire' (he was, of course, referring to the fact that he lived in Windsor Castle).

22.	*Princess (later Queen) Victoria* was brought to Salisbury by both her parents in December 1819, staying in the Bishop's Palace. She was just six months old at the time. The Bishop had been a tutor to Victoria's father, and was so delighted to see his former pupil's baby daughter that he began to toss her playfully into the air. The infant Victoria was not amused, and grabbed the Bishop's wig, which fell off, together with tufts of episcopal hair.

23 & 24.	*Edward VII* and *Queen Alexandra* came to Salisbury in 1908, on their way to Wilton. In thanking the Mayor for the welcome given to himself and the Queen, King Edward said: 'Your noble cathedral, a living monument of the piety of those long dead, attracts visitors from all parts of the world, and is justly famous, as one of the most beautiful places of worship in the country.' It was after this visit that the King's statue was placed in a niche on the High Street Gate.

25.	*Queen Elizabeth II* visited Salisbury Cathedral in April 1974, for the Royal Maundy Service, and presented Maundy Money to eighteen old people in the city.

26.	*Charles, Prince of Wales*, was Patron of the Spire Appeal at the end of the twentieth century, and was present at the celebration concert held in the Close on 29 May 2000.

SEVEN OLD PUBS

Salisbury is richly endowed with pubs – many of them hundreds of years old, with interesting historical associations. These are some of the most famous.

1. *The Haunch of Venison*, in the centre of the city, in Minster Street just opposite the Poultry Cross, is probably the oldest hostelry in Salisbury. The enormous oak beams throughout the building are thought to come from early sailing vessels.

    The first record of the Haunch of Venison is about 1320, when the building was used to house craftsmen working on the cathedral spire. At the back it is right next to St Thomas's Church, and there is a rumour that an underground tunnel ran between church and tavern (then, reputedly, a brothel), so that the clergy could visit without being seen! The various levels in the building were used by clergy according to their status, and the so-called House of Lords, situated on the upper ground floor, was built to accommodate higher clergy orders.

    In addition to the House of Lords, the bar has a small intimate 'Horsebox'. This small bar was originally for ladies to use, and reputedly it was used by Churchill and Eisenhower during the planning of the D-Day landings.

    There are so many things to see and enjoy in the Haunch of Venison, quite apart from its excellent restaurant, 'One'. The tiles in the bar were once a part of the cathedral. The pewter bar top is believed to be the last complete one of its kind in England. The fireplace in the main dining room dates back to 1588 – the year of the Armada. And there is another bar that has the only licensed landing in England.

    Then there is the gruesome severed mummified hand with playing cards, found during restoration work in the nineteenth century. This is thought to have belonged to someone caught cheating at cards. It is now on view in a small recess upstairs. No wonder there are ghostly happenings. For sheer atmosphere, the Haunch of Venison has few pubs to compare with it (see the list of ghosts on page 99).

> A big butcher seated quite near him
> Was growing belligerent and
> Drawing the blade from his scabbard
> He struck off the stranger's right hand.
>
> The man screamed in horror and anguish
> How on earth had the trick been exposed?
> For clutched in the hand in the rushes
> Four aces were clearly disclosed.
>
> (Two verses taken from a locally written ballad
> entitled 'The Hand at the Haunch')

During restoration work at the Haunch of Venison, workmen discovered a gruesome mummified hand with playing cards. Was it someone caught cheating at cards? Probably no one will ever discover the full story. Nevertheless, this hand can still be seen in a wall recess in this popular pub in Minster Street, opposite the Poultry Cross.

2.   *The King's Arms*, in St John Street, almost opposite St Ann's Gate, is a beautiful half-timbered building of four storeys. It has great historical associations, for it was here, in 1651, that royalist supporters of King Charles II, fleeing after defeat at the battle of Worcester, planned the king's escape route to France, ably assisted by the landlord Hewitt.

The inn is full of hiding-places, and there is a secret chamber in the roof, reached through a sliding panel. A seventeenth-century tumbler was found there when the chamber was rediscovered in the nineteenth century.

The King's Arms is one of Salisbury's oldest inns, built shortly after the cathedral itself. Don't miss the 'man-trap' hanging in the ceiling of the entrance into the yard to the left of the building. It is a fearsome reminder of what could happen to trespassers in former centuries.

The King's Arms in St John Street.

THE DEVIL VISITS A SALISBURY PUB, WITH A 'STINKING SAVOUR'

'. . . There was one at Salisbury, in the midst of his health, drinking and carousing in a tavern; and he drank a health to the devil, saying that if the devil would not come and pledge him, he would not believe that there was either God or devil. Whereupon his companions, stricken with fear, hastened out of the room.

. . . presently after, hearing a hideous noise, and smelling a stinking savour, the vintner ran up into the chamber; and coming in he missed his guest, and found the window broken, the iron bar in it bowed, and all bloody. But the man was never heard of afterwards.'

(John Bunyan, *The Life and Death of Mr Badman*, 1680)

(Unfortunately, Bunyan didn't tell us which inn was involved in this incident. Was it The Haunch of Venison? The New Inn? The King's Arms? Sadly, we shall never know.)

3.   *The New Inn*, in New Street – contrary to what its name may suggest – is one of the oldest pubs in Salisbury. As it is built on the south side of New Street, its rear garden is bounded by a section of the Close wall, built in 1341. The view of the cathedral spire from this lovely, secluded garden makes a visit to the New Inn well worth your while, quite apart from the excellent brews and cuisine.

The New Inn, in New Street.

4.   *The Pheasant Inn*, in Salt Lane, dates from the fifteenth century, and it incorporates an ancient guild hall that once belonged to the city's Shoemakers' Guild – indeed, the Pheasant Inn was once known as the Crispin, being named after the patron saint of shoemakers. The hall was once the home of a schoolmaster son of a master shoemaker, and when he died he generously left his house to Salisbury's Company of Shoemakers. By 1821 the inn had changed its name to the Pheasant. Today, the pub makes use of its old guild hall as a attractive function room – appropriately called 'Shoemakers'.

The Pheasant Inn, Salt Lane.

5. *The Red Lion*, in Milford Street, was originally built to house workmen building the new cathedral, and is believed to be the longest-running purpose-built hotel in the country. The original thirteenth-century range is the heart of the present building. It was firmly established by the fifteenth century and became a fine coaching inn in the eighteenth. Its high entrance allowed tall coaches to enter the coaching yard. Hung with Virginia creeper, it is a delightful old hostelry, possessing a grand effigy sign of a red lion.

6. *The Rose and Crown*, in Harnham, is only a short walk from the cathedral, reached by leaving the Close by Harnham Gate. Turn right, cross the bridge over the River Avon, and continue along Harnham Road, until you arrive at the Rose and Crown, with its splendid long half-timbered exterior. The earliest part of this timber-framed building was begun in about 1380. It is situated on the banks of the Avon, and the view of the cathedral across the water meadows from the rose garden is simply superb. Understandably, this is one of the views that John Constable chose to paint when he visited Salisbury in the 1820s.

The Rose and Crown, Harnham, dating from *c.* 1380.

7.   *The White Hart*, in St John Street, with its large effigy sign of a magnificent white hart high on the skyline, is described by Charles Dickens in his novel *Martin Chuzzlewit*, published in 1843. More than two centuries earlier, in 1618, Sir Walter Raleigh, staying in Salisbury after his disastrous final voyage to the New World, obtained food from an earlier White Hart Inn, which stood on this site. The story goes that Sir Walter was desperately afraid of the King's anger, and was busy writing his defence. He tried to buy time for himself by pretending to be ill and unable to eat. Secretly, however, the White Hart was supplying him with 'a leg of mutton and some loaves', which he ate while no one was looking. The present inn was built in the seventeenth century and it has an impressive classical façade added in about 1800.

The White Hart

EMETICS AND NITRIC ACID FOR SIR WALTER RALEIGH

Desperate to buy time for himself and regain the favour of King James, Sir Walter Raleigh passed through Salisbury in 1618, under arrest on his way to London. He lodged somewhere near the White Hart, possibly staying at the King's Arms.

Meanwhile, coincidentally, the King had also come to Salisbury and was staying at the Bishop's Palace in the Close, just a few hundred yards away.

Raleigh's desperate plan to gain a few days' respite from travelling and to win sympathy from the King was to pretend to be seriously ill. His personal doctor agreed to make Sir Walter 'look horrible and loathsome outwardly'. Secretly, he gave Raleigh some powerful emetics and rubbed his arms, legs and body with a mixture containing nitric acid. Almost immediately Raleigh became spectacularly disfigured.

The plan worked, at least for a while, and Raleigh set to work to write his *Apology for the Voyage to Guyana*.

EIGHT AUTHORS

Here are some authors who wrote books while living or staying in Salisbury.

1. *Richard Hooker* (1554–1600), an influential English religious thinker, living in the reign of Queen Elizabeth I. He helped to formulate the faith of the Church of England. He was a subdean and prebendary of the cathedral, and during his time there he wrote the first four books of his *Laws of Ecclesiastical Polity*, publishing them in 1594.

2. Sir Walter Raleigh (1552–1618) stayed in lodgings in Salisbury after his disastrous expedition to Guyana in 1618. While there he wrote his book *Apology for the Voyage to Guyana*. Here he feigned to be ill (see page 87) and unable to take nourishment, but in secret he was still reasonably fit, and desperate to write his account of the Orinoco expedition and justify his actions.

3. *George Herbert* (1593–1633) was one of the greatest religious poets of the seventeenth century. He was the Rector of Bemerton, a village about two miles west of Salisbury, and he wrote much of his poetry in the rectory just opposite the little church of St Andrew. George Herbert enjoyed listening to the music sung in the cathedral, and would walk there once a week to hear it. Afterwards he would visit friends in the Close and take part in music-making with them. His poems have become well-known hymns, including 'Let all the World in every Corner Sing' and 'Teach me, my God and King'.

4. *Gilbert Burnet* (1643–1715) was a highly controversial political churchman who served William of Orange as his chaplain. When William became king, he rewarded Burnet for his loyalty by making him Bishop of Salisbury. In his first pastoral letter Burnet defended William's right to be king by conquest. This offended Parliament so much that it was burned by the public hangman. Gilbert Burnet's best-known book is his detailed account of the English political scene at the end of the seventeenth century, *A History of my Own Time*, written in Salisbury and published in 1724–34.

5. *Henry Fielding* (1707–54) wrote some chapters of *Tom Jones* while he was staying at his mother-in-law's house, 14 The Close. He began the book in the summer of 1746 and completed it towards the end of 1748.

6. *Sir Arthur Bryant* (1899–1985), the historian, lived at Myles Place in the Close, and wrote many of his popular books there.

7. *Leslie Thomas* (b. 1931), the novelist, has written many of his bestsellers at his home, the Walton Canonry, next to Myles Place.

8.   *William Golding* (1911–93) was a young schoolmaster at Bishop Wordsworth's School. He joined the navy in 1940, returned to teaching in 1946 and began writing the remarkable novels that led to his being awarded the Nobel Prize for Literature in 1983. His first notable success, *Lord of the Flies*, brought him so much fame and income that he left his teaching post and devoted himself to full-time writing, still living near Salisbury. His novel *The Spire* is clearly about the building of the spire of Salisbury Cathedral – a fascinatingly imaginative work about the possible motives for undertaking such a daring enterprise. Although it is pure fiction, *The Spire* is essential reading for all who share a love of the cathedral.

William Golding, Nobel prize-winner 1983, who taught at Bishop Wordsworth's School in 1940 and, after war service, from 1946 to 1961.

11 The Close, which is part of Bishop Wordsworth's School. The cathedral immediately behind this building is clearly the inspiration for Golding's novel *The Spire*. One room in this eighteenth-century building was made as the result of a bet between three Salisbury citizens, to see which of them could build the most beautiful room for the entertainment of their guests.

FOUR OLD CHURCHES

I   *St Martin's* is probably the oldest building in Salisbury. A village parish church stood on this site long before Bishop Poore began the new cathedral in the meadows just a few hundred yards to the south. In fact, Bishop Poore, St Osmund and St Edmund would all have known St Martin's and would have worshipped here. Of course, the building has seen many changes, and its chancel was rebuilt in the Early English style just before the cathedral itself was begun.

Among the many interesting features are its thirteenth-century Purbeck marble font; an exceptionally fine eagle lectern; the Swayne monument in white and grey marble, possibly by Rysbrack; another memorial (to John and Margaret Blake) by Flaxman; a banner by Sir Ninian Comper; and, dominating the interior, a magnificent great rood screen spanning the chancel arch. The Hill organ is considered to be the finest in Salisbury after the cathedral. A curiosity is a fifteenth-century carving of a woman, possibly a nun, wearing spectacles – very much a trend-setting invention at that time.

St Martin's is reached by walking up St Ann's Street and taking the underpass to Tollgate Road.

Fifteenth-century carving in St Martin's, depicting a woman wearing spectacles.

A TWENTIETH-CENTURY MIRACLE?

St Martin's was the scene, in 1938, of what many believed to be an astonishing miracle. In that year, the curate was talking to a blind toymaker, a Mr Edginton, and during their conversation he described the chancel of St Martin's. Mr Edginton was a skilled craftsman despite his blindness, and was fascinated by the curate's description – perhaps of the intricately carved rood screen.

That night Mr Edginton dreamed about the chancel and imagined that he saw it as the curate had described. He felt an overpowering urge to go there. He asked the curate to accompany him and when they got into the church they both knelt down to pray. Suddenly, the blind man experienced a flash of light, and to his amazement he found that he was able to see the chancel. Looking round, he could see the curate and the sexton. Trembling with excitement he went home and – incredibly – saw his wife for the first time!

2.   *St Edmund's*, in Bedwin Street in the north of the city, was dedicated in the name of St Edmund Rich (1170–1240), who had been Treasurer of the cathedral while it was built, and in whose memory St Edmund Hall, Oxford, was founded. St Edmund's Church was founded by Bishop de la Wyle in 1269. Its former tower fell down in 1653, so, unusually, the present tower was built in Cromwellian days.

A few years before, Henry Sherfield, a Puritanical fanatic, threw a brick through one of the stained glass windows in St Edmund's Church, complaining that the scene of the Creation depicted there was chronologically incorrect, and said that he thought God looked undignified as 'a little old man in a long blue coat' and 'it is moreover very darksome whereby such as sit near the same [window] cannot read in their books'.

In St Edmund's churchyard in 1771, according to the *Antiquarian and Topographical Cabinet* published in 1811, 'the mouldering bones of nearly thirty bodies, several pikeheads, a large iron sword, and several other warlike implements were found here'. Those who dug up these remains were convinced that the churchyard had been 'the scene of a sanguinary battle'. They even wondered whether it was the site of the famous battle fought by Cynric against the ancient Britons (see page 1) – but probably no one will ever know the real facts.

The seventeenth-century Cromwellian tower of St Edmund's. Oliver Cromwell would be amazed to know that this church is now a thriving and popular arts centre.

SALISBURY ARTS CENTRE – ST EDMUND'S NEW ROLE

St Edmund's has now been turned into a highly successful and vibrant arts centre. The facilities for a wide range of artistic activities are being wonderfully upgraded, thanks to funding by the Arts Council England, the Heritage Lottery Fund, Salisbury District Council and many other generous donors. This newly refurbished arts complex opened in 2005, at a total cost of over four million pounds.

3.

St Andrew's is in the village of Bemerton on the western outskirts of Salisbury. Its origins go back to the fourteenth century. Today it is a beautiful, quiet, unpretentious little building where the presence of George Herbert can still be felt. He was rector of the parish from 1630 to 1633, and it was in the rectory just opposite the church that he wrote most of his poems and his prose work *The Country Parson*, a set of reflections on how priests should live and work.

George Herbert is buried by the altar. A stained glass window at the west end of the church shows Herbert in one panel and his friend Nicholas Ferrar of Little Gidding in the other. Ferrar is depicted with a manuscript in his hand – the poems of George Herbert, which Herbert gave him to publish after his death. George Herbert himself is shown with the cathedral in the background and carrying his lute – an early form of stringed instrument something like a guitar or mandolin. He used to walk every week to the Close to make music with his friends.

St Andrew's Church, Bemerton, where George Herbert was rector.

THE COUNTRY PARSON

'The Country Parson hath special care of his Church, that all things there be decent and befitting his Name, by which it is called. Therefore, First, he takes order, that all things be in good repair; as walls plastered, windows glazed, floor paved, seats whole, firm, and uniform, especially that the Pulpit, and Desk, and Communion Table, and Font be as they ought, for those great duties that are performed in them. Secondly, That the Church be swept clean without dust, or Cobwebs, and at great Festivals strewed and stuck with boughs, and perfumed with incense.'

(George Herbert, The Country Parson)

Stained-glass window in St Andrew's Church, Bemerton, showing George Herbert and his friend Nicholas Ferrar, of Little Gidding.

'LET ALL THE WORLD'

Let all the world in every corner sing,
    My God and King!
    The heavens are not too high,
    His praise may thither fly;
    The earth is not too low,
    His praises there may grow.
Let all the world in every corner sing,
    My God and King!

Let all the world in every corner sing,
    My God and King!
    The Church with psalms must shout,
    No door can keep them out;
    But, above all, the heart
    Must bear the longest part.
Let all the world in every corner sing,
    My God and King!

(George Herbert, 1593–1633)

4.　　*St Thomas's* was one of the very first buildings to be put in the City of New Sarum. It was originally made of wood, and was specially built as a place of worship for the workmen who were camping in the nearby meadows, busy constructing the new cathedral. It has been altered and enlarged many times over the centuries. It is dedicated to St Thomas Becket, whose bones were translated from the crypt of Canterbury Cathedral to a magnificent new shrine before the high altar of Canterbury Cathedral, exactly ten weeks after the foundation stones of Salisbury Cathedral were laid. And, importantly, the man who supervised both these major events was Elias de Dereham. The dedication of Salisbury's little wooden chapel to Thomas Becket must have been charged with significance in the minds of those early worshippers.

The tower of St Thomas's, showing the clock jacks (above). This view is to be seen from the small passage alongside the Haunch of Venison pub in Minster Street.

EIGHT THINGS TO BE SEEN IN ST THOMAS'S CHURCH

1. *The Doom Painting*, painted on the chancel arch, dominates the interior. This was painted about 1475, whitewashed over at the Reformation, and then rediscoved and restored in the nineteenth century. This fascinating painting is believed to be the largest wall-painting of the Last Judgement still surviving. It is described in detail on page 97.

2. *Nearly 250 angels* are carved in wood and stone throughout the Church – on the walls, pillars, and high up in the roof. How many can you find ?

3. *St George's altar* is formed from a beautiful late medieval tomb of a member of the Godmanstone family. It bears their merchant's mark on its central shield. A Godmanstone, when Mayor, built this side of the church, and included a Guild Chapel of St George for the Mayor and Corporation.

4. *The Royal arms of Queen Elizabeth I* hangs on the south wall. Interestingly, it shows the Tudor Dragon instead of the Scottish Unicorn.

5. *The Lady Chapel*, rededicated in 1984 to Our Lady and St Edmund, was built in 1470 by William Swayne, a Mayor of Salisbury and a rich wool merchant, both for his family and also for the Tailors' Guild.

6. *The Georgian organ* was originally presented by George III in 1792 to Salisbury Cathedral as his personal gift, adding to the 'improvements' of James Wyatt. The organ was given by the Dean and Chapter to St Thomas's in 1877.

7. *The heraldic funeral hatchments*, hanging high up on the walls, comprise a set of seventeenth- and eighteenth-century wooden 'achievements', of distinguished families of St Thomas's and St Edmund's parishes, each displaying the armorial bearings of the deceased person.

8. *The clock jacks*, high up on the exterior of the east side of the tower, are shown on the opposite page. These are colourful carvings of two little men who strike bells every quarter of an hour. These were restored to working order in 1983. To see them, you need to turn left as you leave the church, walk round the block into Minster Street, and go to the end of a little passage beside the Haunch of Venison. (See page 82 for an interesting speculation about a connection between St Thomas's and the pub.)

The Doom Painting in St Thomas's Church.

THIRTEEN DETAILS OF DOOM

The Doom Painting, pictured opposite, is acknowledged to be the finest in the country. It was painted in about 1475, and shows Christ on the Day of Judgement sending the souls of the righteous to Heaven and the souls of the wicked to Hell. This analysis may help to appreciate the details more clearly.

1.   *Christ in Majesty* is seen at the top, sitting on one rainbow, with his feet resting on another. His hands are raised in blessing and his five bleeding wounds are clearly depicted.

2.   *An angel holding a T-shaped cross* is next to Jesus on the left of the picture. On the cross hangs Christ's crown of thorns. The angel also holds the three nails.

3.   *An angel holding a pillar* is next to Jesus on the right of the picture. This is the pillar on which Jesus was scourged. The angel also holds a spear and a sponge.

4.   *The Twelve Apostles* are seated in a row just below Jesus' feet.

5.   *The Virgin Mary* is on the left, just above the first of the Apostles.

6.   *St John the Evangelist* is on the right, just above the last of the Apostles.

7.   *Souls of the Righteous* are shown on the left of the picture, rising out of their graves and being guided to Heaven by winged angels. They are all naked, but one of these is a man with a mitre on his head, to indicate that he was a bishop.

8.   *Souls of the Damned* are shown on the right of the picture being dragged and thrust into Hell.

9.   *The Prince of Darkness* presides over this side, and he is dramatically identified by having his clawed foot projecting out of the picture over the edge of the chancel arch. He has the horned head of a beast.

10.   *The 'dishonest ale-wife'* is next to the Prince of Darkness, holding a jug in her hand. A devil is grasping her in his arms. The ale-wife is shown fully clothed, and her dress helps us to date the painting to the late fifteenth century.

11.   *A group of damned souls, chained together,* are being dragged down the mouth of Hell. Notice that one of these wears a bishop's mitre, and two others wear crowns.

12.   *The mouth of hell* gapes wide, like that of a huge dragon. It is being held open by two horned devils.

13.   *A miser* is shown just below the mouth of Hell, carrying money bags. He is being dragged by another devil and he has black burn-marks on his shoulder where the devil has touched him with his claws.

The large figure at the bottom of the left-hand side is *St James*, the Patron Saint of pilgrims, wearing a scallop shell in his hat. The large figure at the bottom of the right-hand side is thought to be *St Osmund*, Patron Saint of Salisbury, canonised in 1457 (see pages 38–9).

Finally, the scroll just above St Osmund reads 'Nulla est Redemptio', which can roughly be translated as 'There's no escape for the wicked'.

TWELVE PEOPLE PUT TO DEATH

In earlier centuries, executions, hangings and burnings were carried out in public, providing horrific entertainment and warning to the citizens. Here are some of the victims of the death penalty in Salisbury.

1. *The Duke of Buckingham* was executed in Salisbury marketplace in 1483 for treason against Richard III (Shakespeare's 'hunchback'). A plaque on the wall outside Debenham's store marks the spot near which this execution took place.

Plaque on the front of Debenham's store in Blue Boar Row.

2. *Lord Stourton* was hanged in the marketplace for murder in 1556. Queen Mary I ('Bloody Mary') refused the usual grace of the Crown, which was to allow noblemen to be beheaded instead of hanged. She ordered him to die at the gallows like a common criminal. However, Lord Stourton was determined to die like a gentleman, so a silken cord was used for his noble neck. This silk noose hung upon his tomb in the cathedral for more than two centuries, until it disappeared in 1773.

3. *A condemned felon* threw a brickbat at the magistrates who were sentencing him. The court records describe this incident in an extraordinary mixture of English, French and Latin:

   'Richardson, Chief Justice, at Salisbury, in summer 1631 fuit assault per prisoner condemne pur felony, que puis son condemnation ject a brickbat a le dit justice que narrowly mist. Et pur ceo immediately fuit indictment pur Noy enver le prisoner, et son dexter manus amputee and fixe al gibbet, sur que luy meme immediatement hange in presence de Court.'

4. *A teenager,* aged 15, was hanged, drawn and quartered in 1632 merely for saying he was going to buy a pistol to kill the king (Charles I).

5. *An eighty-year-old witch,* Anne Bodenham, a clothier's wife, was reported to have five spirits at her beck and call, in the guise of little ragged boys. Imprudently, she turned herself into a cat. Not surprisingly, she was convicted of witchcraft and executed.

SEVEN PROTESTANT MARTYRS BURNED TO DEATH IN 1536

John Maundrel, William and Alice Moberley, and John Spicer were all burned together at two stakes in March 1556, for holding Protestant beliefs during the reign of Queen Mary. It was recorded that they 'most constantly gave their bodies to the fire, and their souls to the Lord for the testimony of His truth'. Three wandering minstrels were also burned to death for their beliefs.

NINE GHOSTS DWELLING IN SALISBURY

There are scores of reputed ghosts in Salisbury, and the Tourist Information Office organises popular Ghost Walks led by Blue Guides on certain evenings. Here are just a few of the spirits who make their presence felt in the city.

1. *The Duke of Buckingham*, friend turned enemy of Richard III, was executed in a courtyard behind Debenham's store in Blue Boar Row. Over the centuries, countless mysterious happenings have occurred on this site. The most spectacular recent event was in June 2002, when all security alarms were set off and all locked doors were flung wide open. Certain areas in the premises have a 'feeling of evil' and fire-watchers would never stay there at night during the Second World War.

2. *'Matilda'* is a teenage ghost who inhabits the last shop on the right along Blue Boar row as you look at Debenham's. It is believed that she died of diphtheria, and that she is particularly interested in fashion.

3. *A lady in Edwardian dress* haunts the shop next door to the left of the shop where 'Matilda' dwells. One day, just as the shop had closed, she emerged through locked doors towards the proprietor and then proceeded to walk straight through him.

4. *'Oliver'* is active in John a'Port's House (Watson's glass and china shop) in Queen Street. A cavalier with a red plumed hat, he is apparently very fussy about how things are displayed in the shop and is likely to move them about.

5. *A smell* of newly dug earth is associated with the ghost who dwells in the Haunch of Venison pub in Minster Street. Here there is a room where a female figure, wearing a mantilla, paces back and forth in distress, dragging her feet. Just below, is a churchyard filled with graves. Some years ago, when alterations were being made to the walls of this pub, a human hand was discovered, together with playing-cards. Visitors to the pub can still see a spine-chilling object on permanent view there (see page 83).

6. *A lady in grey* moves about in a first-floor room in a building on the west side of the Close known as the Wardrobe – now the home of the military museum of the Royal Gloucestershire, Berkshire and Wiltshire Regiment.

7. *A headless cavalier on a horse* has been seen fording the river behind the King's House in the Close, now the Salisbury and South Wiltshire Museum.

8. *A 'dusting ghost'* does its household chores in a house near St Ann's Gate – but confines its activities to dusting only the first-floor rooms, not those on the ground floor. The owners have tested this by leaving chalk dust on surfaces around the house – but invariably the ghost chooses to work only in the upstairs areas !

9. *A friendly ghost* dwells in the house opposite the dusting ghost. It is the former home of Dr Turbeville, the famous seventeenth-century eye doctor. The ghost helped to guide the owner to legal documents hidden in a wall, after which some business contained in those papers was satisfactorily completed. It has exuded a warm and friendly atmosphere in that room ever since.

Part of the 'Drainage Collection' displayed in Salisbury museum.

The items in the 'Drainage Collection' were found in the old canals as they were finally being filled in during the nineteenth century. The collection can be categorised under six headings:

1.   The home: about 450 keys, some dating back to the thirteenth century; cutlery; knives, spoons, forks, shears, scissors, razors.

2.   Dress and personal: buckles, cloak fasteners, clay pipes, pipeclay hair-curlers, purse frames, brooches, rings, seals, toys and a beautiful fourteenth-century chess-piece made from walrus ivory.

3.   Tools: thimbles, needles, pins, scissors, saddlers' knives, carpenters' and stonemasons' tools, and an eighteenth-century silver bo'sun's call.

4.   The Church: pilgrims' badges, crucifixes, ampullae (small flasks for holy water or oil), rings, papal seals.

5.   Horse equipment: horseshoes, spurs, stirrups, bits, buckles, bells, saddle-pommels, heraldic trappings.

6.   Weapons: arrowheads, pieces of chainmail, daggers, quillons (hand guards), spearheads, gun locks.

SIX THINGS TO SEE IN THE MUSEUM

The Salisbury and South Wiltshire Museum is in the King's House, only a few minutes' walk away from the West Front of the cathedral. It is crammed with all kinds of fascinating items. Here are six favourites.

1. *Stuffed bustards*. Great bustards were huge birds that once lived on Salisbury Plain. They could weigh up to 50lb and the largest had a wing span of 7ft. They were hunted to extinction in England. One of the last, on view here, with a wing span of 62in, was shot in 1871 (see illustration below). The then curator, Frank Stevens, sat down with nine other people to enjoy its meat. It is good to report that in 2004 specially incubated bustards from Russia were reintroduced to live on Salisbury Plain. Forty chicks will be imported annually for the next five to ten years, until the bustard population is large enough to sustain itself.

2. *A prehistoric skeleton*. This skeleton, clutching a beaker, is part of an impressive display concerning Stonehenge and the people who lived on Salisbury Plain, known as the Beaker Folk, in prehistoric times.

3. *Hob Nob and the Giant St Christopher*. These dramatic figures never fail to capture children's imaginations (see following spread for more details).

4. *The drainage collection*. When the old canals were filled in, after the terrible outbreaks of typhus in the nineteenth century, all kinds of objects were found: keys, combs, coins, scissors, knives. What is known as the 'Drainage Collection' gives a unique insight into the lives of former Salisbury citizens.

5. *Model of Old Sarum* giving a good impression of what the old city looked like before the cathedral was transferred to its present site.

6. *Doctor's surgery* of the 1930s – not so long ago and within memory of older visitors – very nostalgic to those who can remember the time before the NHS.

The group of great bustards on view in Salisbury museum. Having become extinct in England in the nineteenth century, they were reintroduced on Salisbury Plain in 2004.

ONE GIANT, TWO WHIFFLERS AND HOB-NOB

Two striking objects in Salisbury Museum are the *Giant St Christopher* and his companion, a wooden horse with ferocious snapping jaws, called *Hob-Nob*.

The giant stands fourteen feet from the ground, and is made of a hollow, light wooden frame covered with a red woollen robe. He wears a fifteenth-century style head-dress, and a pair of leather gauntlets. Over his shoulder is a leather belt in which he carried his lion-hilted wooden sword.

The belt is decorated with the arms of the Salisbury Guild of Tailors, who originally owned him and carried him in procession every year on 23 June, the Eve of the nativity of St John the Baptist, their patron saint. One man inside the giant can carry him – perhaps somewhat gingerly – whenever he moves in stately procession through the streets of Salisbury.

Guild effigies such as these were quite common in England during the Middle Ages, but almost all of them were destroyed at the time of the reformation. Two similar famous giant figures were Gog and Magog in London's Guildhall, but when these were destroyed in the blitz, their destruction meant that Salisbury's Giant St Christopher is now the only remaining ancient guild effigy in the country.

His companion, *Hob-Nob*, accompanies the giant whenever he parades the streets of Salisbury. Hob-Nob is hollow, draped with black cloth decorated with the arms of the Merchant Tailors' Guild, and the man inside can work Hob-Nob's snapping jaws, chasing and teasing the onlookers, sometimes tearing their clothes, and generally creating mayhem. In the Middle Ages he chivvied apprentices into the old canals.

The giant and Hob-Nob are still brought out in procession through Salisbury streets to celebrate important national events such as coronations, jubilees and anniversaries. Traditionally, they are also accompanied by Morris dancers, a yeoman or beadle to carry his staff of office, and *two whifflers*. One of these splendidly named characters carries a 'mace' – a kind of imitation lantern carried on a long pole; and the other carries an enormous wooden sword.

Much has been written about these unique survivals from a distant past. Obviously they are both linked with ancient tradition and folklore, but their exact significance can only be guessed at. Certainly they are two of the most popular items in today's museum.

The Giant and Hob-Nob, accompanied by his two whifflers and a beadle. This photograph was taken in St Ann Street in 1887.

'GROVELY, GROVELY, GROVELY'

A curious ceremony is held around the cathedral on 29 May – Oak Apple Day – and clearly this has links with a pagan past when the Green Man figured in pre-Christian tree-worship rituals.

In Wishford, a village about six miles west of Salisbury, the custom of cutting oak boughs from trees in nearby Grovely Woods has existed from 'time out of mind'. Wishford villagers have a legal right to 'collect dead wood all the year round and cut green boughs on Oak Apple Day'.

The ceremonies begin before dawn, as dustbin lids, bells, trumpets and the traditional cry of 'Grovely, Grovely, Grovely and all Grovely' wake the folk of Wishford, rousing them to go to the woods. Traditionally, the boughs they then cut from the oak trees must be no larger than the thickness of a man's forearm. Attractively shaped branches are preferred – those that resemble a deer's antlers – and also the boughs should bear 'oak apples' – the curious little brown marble-shaped growths that are formed by gall wasps. Any countryman knows what oak apples are: they are quite different from acorns, which are the true seed of the oak.

Oak-apple gatherers from Wishford dancing in front of the Cathedral in 1956.

Oak-apple gatherers assembling in the Close on May Day, c. 2000. Mompesson House is in the background. Note their banner, inscribed with the traditional Grovely shout.

Having collected a goodly supply of oak branches, the villagers then use some of them to decorate the church and their houses. They then enjoy a hearty breakfast, after which they proceed to Salisbury Cathedral with the rest of their oak apple boughs. In former years they used to dance and revel all the way to the cathedral, but nowadays they use easier transport. Some dress themselves in early nineteenth-century costume.

Having arrived at the Close, they dance with oak twigs and 'nitches' – bundles of dry wood – in front of the cathedral, after which the whole gathering, with banners and oak boughs, go into the cathedral for a service; oak branches are placed on the altar, and again the traditional cry of 'Grovely, Grovely, Grovely and all Grovely' is shouted with joyful acclaim.

Surely no other cathedral witnesses such a scene. The pagan past still lives vividly in Salisbury on 'Oak Apple Day.'

EIGHT NOTABLE BUILDINGS IN SALISBURY

This half-timbered building is opposite Mitre House in High Street. It dates back to the fourteenth century. For more than half a century it was well known as Beach's Bookshop, but it is now a popular restaurant.

The top bay windows of the former George Inn, in the High Street. Many famous people have stayed at The George, including Oliver Cromwell and Samuel Pepys.

William Russel's house in Queen Street – often referred to as the House of John a' Port. It is the oldest datable timber-framed building in Salisbury, dating back to the early fourteenth century. A deed of 1306 gave William Russel, a wool merchant, this piece of land. It is now Watson's china and glass shop – the firm has been in business since 1834.

Mitre House in High Street is traditionally the site of the first house in Salisbury, where Bishop Poore lived while the cathedral was being built. Note the bishop's mitre on the wall. A Salisbury custom is that a newly appointed bishop always robes himself in Mitre House just before going to the Cathedral to be enthroned.

Church House in Crane Bridge Street is now a beautiful, tranquil building on the bank of the River Avon. It was formerly the home of a wealthy merchant. It became the city's workhouse in 1638 and this was its use for more than 200 years – 'a scene of filth and misrule'. It now belongs to the Church of England, and houses administrative offices of the diocese.

St Nicholas Hospital. The College of St Nicholas de Vaux, founded by Bishop Bridport in 1261 for twenty 'poor, needy, honourable and teachable scholars'. Students came from Oxford to form a thriving university here in the thirteenth and fourteenth centuries. Later it became an almshouse and it was while standing on Harnham Bridge in 1851, looking at this building, that Anthony Trollope was inspired to write *The Warden*, set in the cathedral city of Barchester.

The Odeon cinema, in New Canal, obviously has a fake medieval façade. However, as soon as you enter it, you quickly realise that the interior is genuine. Its impressive entrance hall with a superb timber roof is the hall of John Halle, a rich wool merchant, four times mayor of Salisbury in the fifteenth century (see p. 120). Even the fake façade is interesting, for it was designed by Augustus Pugin, creator of the decorations throughout the Houses of Parliament. Pugin lived near Salisbury and also designed St Osmund's Church in Exeter Street.

The Clock Tower in Fisherton Street was built in 1893 by a Salisbury physician, Dr Roberts, as a memorial to his wife. It stands on the site of the old city gaol and it is worth walking all round the base to note the carvings, and the bars on an old window facing the river. In medieval times the river marked the boundary between the city of Salisbury and the parish of Fisherton Anger.

SIXTEEN BOOKS ABOUT THE CITY AND CATHEDRAL

Anyone wanting to know more about various aspects of the cathedral – stained glass, masons' marks, Magna Carta, the medieval clock, etc. – is advised to browse in the cathedral shop, situated in the cloisters. Here, there is a constant supply of beautifully produced pamphlets and books not readily available elsewhere. Also there is an excellent collection of books and pamphlets in the reception area of the Salisbury and South Wilts Museum, opposite the West Front of the cathedral. Nationally, the following books are warmly recommended:

1. Brown, Sarah, *Sumptuous and Richly Adorn'd: The Decoration of Salisbury Cathedral* (The Stationery Office, 1999)

2. Burnett, David, *Salisbury, The History of an English Cathedral City* (Compton Press, c. 1980)

3. Chadwick, John C., *The Unusual Guide to Salisbury* (Nigel Clarke Publications, 1986)

4. Chandler, John, *Endless Street, A History of Salisbury and its People* (Hobnob, 1983)

5. Chandler, John, *A Salisbury Assortment* (Ex Libris Press, 1996)

6. Chandler, John, *Salisbury: History and Guide* (Alan Sutton Publishing, 1992)

7. Evans, Sydney, *Salisbury Cathedral: A Reflective Guide* (Michael Russell, 1985)

8. Fletcher, Revd J.M.J., *The Story of Salisbury Cathedral* (Raphael Tuck & Sons Ltd, 1933)

9. Hudson, W.H., *A Shepherd's Life* (Methuen, 1910)

10. Newman, Ruth, and Howells, Jane, *Salisbury Past* (Phillimore, 2001)

11. Robertson, Dora H., *Sarum Close. A History of the Life and Education of the Cathedral Choristers for 700 Years* (Jonathan Cape, 1938)

12. Sharp, Thomas, *Newer Sarum: A Plan for Salisbury* (Architectural Press, 1949)

13. Shortt, Hugh (ed.), *Salisbury: A New Approach to the City and its Neighbourhood* (Salisbury and District Preservation Trust, 1972)

14. Spring, R., *Salisbury Cathedral* (New Bell's Cathedral Guides, 1987)

15. Truby, Jeffrey, *The Glories of Salisbury Cathedral* (Winchester Publications Ltd, 1948)

16. White, Gleeson (ed.), *Salisbury, The Cathedral and City* (George Bell & Sons, 1896)

THREE STATUES

1. *Walking Madonna*. On the lawn surrounding the cathedral and facing visitors as they enter the Close from the High Street Gate is an impressively powerful statue by Elisabeth Frink entitled *Walking Madonna*. It is a lifesize bronze sculpture of the Virgin Mary striding purposefully towards the city. It was placed here in 1981, a timeless reminder of the woman to whom the cathedral is dedicated.

2. *Edward VII*. High up in a niche above the arch of the High Street Gate is a surprising little statue of Edward VII (1901–10), son of Queen Victoria. It is a replacement of an earlier statue, possibly that of James I (1603–25), who was popular in Salisbury because he granted the city its charter of incorporation in 1612. But even before this there had been a statue of Henry III (reigned 1216–72), who had provided timber for the construction of the cathedral and who had been present at its consecration in 1258.

3. *Henry Fawcett*. In the market square, facing Blue Boar Row, is a statue of one of Salisbury's most remarkable citizens, Henry Fawcett (1833–84). He was a leading member of Gladstone's government, and an innovative and successful Postmaster General – a remarkable achievement, considering that he was totally blind. He had lost his sight in a shooting accident as a teenager, shot by his own father.

    Despite his blindness, he became a brilliant student at Cambridge, where he was appointed Professor of Political Economy. Entering politics in 1863, he rose to become Postmaster General, and completely revised the country's archaic postal system. He founded the parcel post, invented postal orders, began cheap telegrams and initiated the Savings Bank scheme.

    His statue looks directly across the road to the site of his father's draper's shop, where he was born. Nowadays it is a Debenham's store.

Walking Madonna by Elisabeth Frink.

Statue of Edward VII on the High Street Gate.

Statue of Henry Fawcett in Salisbury marketplace.

FIVE CURIOSITIES

Mantrap in the roof of the entrance of the backyard of the King's Arms in St John's Street (see page 84)

Marks on the exterior south wall of the cloisters, seen from the Close. These were made by Cromwellian soldiers practising shooting cannon balls at the cathedral.

Oxford University coat of arms, on De Vaux House, in De Vaux Place, commemorating the site where Oxford students, coming to Salisbury, formed a university.

Above, right: One of six grotesque carvings of bewhiskered figures with enormous breasts, found on the front of the Joiners' Hall in St Ann Street.

Right: Sundial on the side of Malmesbury House, just inside St Ann's Gate into the Close.

PART FOUR

Facts and Knowhow for Visitors

TWO ESSENTIAL WEBSITES AND ADDRESSES

1.   www.visitsalisbury.com.

   This is the website of the Salisbury Tourist Information Centre which is at the back of the Guildhall.
   Fish Row, Salisbury, Wiltshire, SP1 1EJ
   tel: 01722 334956 · email: visitorinfo@salisbury.gov.uk

   This essential website about Salisbury gives details of everything a visitor needs to know about modern Salisbury and the surrounding area: Accommodation Guide; Regional Maps; Getting About; Tourist Information Centres; Places to Visit; Sport and Leisure Activities; Towns and Villages; Conferences and Meetings; Music, Theatre, Dance, Culture, Fun; Learning English; Shops and Shopping; and Eating Out.
   The Tourist Information Centre also sells maps, guides, stamps, souvenirs, etc.; it organises City Centre Walks and Ghost Walks; and it sells tickets for events in Salisbury and further afield.

2.   www.salisburycathedral.org.uk.

   This website, updated daily, covers everything of interest about the history and present-day activities of the cathedral; its sections are: Home; Cathedral History and Floor-Plan; Reflections; Services; Visitor Information; Events; News; Education.

   General Enquiries: The Chapter Office, 6 The Close, Salisbury, SP1 2EF
   tel: 01722 555100 · email: chapter@salcath.co.uk

   Visitor Services Dept: tel: 01722 555120 · email: visitors@salcath.co.uk

Consecration Cross in the
Trinity Chapel.

EIGHT TOP HISTORICAL PLACES
TO VISIT IN SALISBURY

1. *Salisbury Cathedral:* www.salisburycathedral.org.uk

   The Chapter Office, 6 The Close, Salisbury, Wiltshire, SP1 2EF
   tel: 01722 555100 · email: chapter@salcath.co.uk

2. *Salisbury and South Wiltshire Museum:* www.salisburymuseum.org.uk

   The King's House, 65 The Close, Salisbury, Wiltshire, SP1 2EN
   tel: 01722 332151 · email: museum@salisburymuseum.org.uk

3. *Redcoats in the Wardrobe Museum:* www.thewardrobe.org.uk

   The Royal Gloucestershire, Berkshire and Wiltshire Regiment Museum, 58 The Close, Salisbury,
   Wiltshire, SP1 2EX
   tel: 01722 419419

4. *Mompesson House:* www.nationaltrust.org.uk

   The Cathedral Close, Salisbury, Wiltshire, SP1 2EX
   tel: 01722 335659

5. *St Thomas's Church:* www.stthomassalisbury.co.uk

   St Thomas House, Salisbury, Wiltshire, SP1 1BA
   tel: 01722 322547 (Parish Office) · email: stcs@fish.co.uk

6. *The Medieval Hall:* www.medieval-hall.co.uk

   The Medieval Hall, Cathedral Close, Salisbury, Wiltshire, SP1 2EX
   tel: 01722 412472 · email: medieval.hall@ntlworld.com

7. *Old Sarum Castle:* www.english-heritage.org.uk

   Castle Road, Salisbury, Wiltshire (about 1½ miles north of Salisbury city centre, off A345)
   tel: 01722 335398 · email: customers@english-heritage.org.uk

8. *Salisbury Arts Centre:* www.salisburyartscentre.co.uk

   St Edmund's Church, Bedwin Street, Salisbury, Wiltshire, SP1 3UT
   tel: 01722 321744

EIGHT TOP NON-HISTORICAL PLACES
TO ENJOY IN SALISBURY

1. *The Maltings Shopping Centre.* Very central, adjoining the Central car Park (1000 spaces) and with a restaurant and pub which occupies a listed building – the Old City Mill.

2. *Salisbury Charter Market.* Dating back to the thirteenth century, the huge marketplace in the centre of Salisbury has an immense range of stalls, selling everything from smoked trout and flowers to jewellery and sausages. Every Tuesday and Saturday (except the third Tuesday in October).

3. *The George Shopping Mall.* Developed on the site of the old George Hotel with entrances from High Street, New Canal and Catherine Street and adjoining the New Street Car Park.

4. *Salisbury Playhouse.* Presenting a wide range of fine quality drama. Situated near the Maltings Shopping Centre and its large car park. Excellent bar and restaurant facilities. Address: Salisbury Playhouse, Malthouse Lane, Salisbury, Wiltshire, SP2 7RA. tel: 01722 320333 (Box Office); 01722 320117 (Admin.) www.salisburyplayhouse.com

5. *City Hall Entertainment Centre.* This is next to the Salisbury Playhouse, hosting many national touring shows, catering for all ages and tastes. Good entertainment at a reasonable price. tel: 01722 434434 www.cityhallsalisbury.co.uk

6. *Creasey Collection of Contemporary Art.* Centrally situated in Salisbury Library and Galleries, Market Place, Salisbury. A changing exhibition of work from the Creasey Collection of Contemporary Art, which includes pictures and sculptures by leading modern artists. tel: 01722 410614

7. *Five Rivers Leisure Centre and Swimming Pool.* A large complex of leisure needs under one roof. New swimming pool, opened in 2002. Refurbished fitness suite, an exciting range of facilities for all ages. Hulse Road, Salisbury, Wiltshire. tel: 01722 339966 www.salisbury.gov.uk/leisure/five-rivers

8. *The Guilder Centre.* Health and Fitness Complex and Physiotherapy and Sports Injury Clinic. Well equipped gym. Alternative therapies: Yoga and Acupuncture. Dance Studio. 16a–18 Guilder Lane, Salisbury, Wiltshire, SP1 1HP. tel: 01722 421404 www.guildercentre.co.uk

FIVE PLACES OF HISTORIC INTEREST
WITHIN TEN MILES OF SALISBURY

1.   *Breamore House and Museum.* A beautiful manor house completed in 1583, containing collections of paintings, furniture, needlework and porcelain. A countryside museum, children's playground, refreshments, etc. 8 miles south of Salisbury off the A338.
     tel: 01725 512468. Nearby is the famous Mizmaze.

2.   *Rockbourne Roman Villa.* The remains of the largest Roman villa in the area, together with a modern museum. Remarkable mosaic floor. 9 miles south of Salisbury, off the A338.
     tel: 01722 518541 www.hants.gov.uk/museum/rockbourne

3.   *Stonehenge.* This World Heritage Site is 9½ miles north of Salisbury, 2 miles west of Amesbury on the junction of A303 and A344/360.
     tel: 01980 624715 www.english-heritage.org.uk/stonehenge

4.   *Wilton House.* Home of the Earl of Pembroke. This is one of the finest country houses in Britain, and contains many splendid state rooms, hung with world-famous paintings, including works by Van Dyck, Reynolds, Brueghel and Rembrandt. Extensive parkland, Palladian bridge, Millennium Water Feature, Rose and Water Gardens. An excellent adventure playground for children and a good restaurant. Four miles west of Salisbury on the A30.
     tel: 01722 746729 www.wiltonhouse.com

5.   *Woodhenge.* Neolithic monument dating from about 2300 BC, with concrete markers replacing the original timbers aligned in six concentric rings, marking the Midsummer sunrise. Less well known than Stonehenge and less spectacular than Avebury, it is nevertheless an interesting ancient 'henge'. 9 miles north of Salisbury, 1½ miles north of Amesbury, just south of Durrington. No facilities; open at any reasonable time; free. You will usually be quite alone as you visit Woodhenge.

Stonehenge, a world heritage site within half-an-hour's drive of Salisbury.

TEN PEOPLE TO THANK
FOR SALISBURY CATHEDRAL

1. *William the Conqueror* – for moving the bishop's throne from Sherborne in Dorset to Old Sarum in Wiltshire.

2. *Bishop Richard Poore* – for moving the bishop's throne from windswept Old Sarum to 'Myrfield' beside the River Avon.

3. *Alice Brewer* – for giving twelve years' supply of Chilmark stone, amounting to 60,000 tons of material for the cathedral.

4. *Elias de Dereham* – for his work in designing the new cathedral and, as the first Clerk of Works, overseeing its construction.

5. *Nicholas of Ely* – for his work as master mason, working closely with Elias de Dereham in supervising and organising work on the cathedral in its early years.

6. *Richard of Farleigh* – for, traditionally, overseeing the building of the spire.

7. *Bishop Richard Beauchamp* – for ordering the bracing arches to be built on the north and south sides of the crossing, thus ensuring that the tower and spire would not collapse.

8. *Sir Christopher Wren* – for surveying the cathedral and designing extra metal 'bandages' to strengthen the fabric still further.

9. *Roy Spring* – Clerk of Works 1968–96 – for his indefatigable work in organising the major survey and subsequent restoration work in the last decades of the twentieth century.

10. *Charles, Prince of Wales* – for giving royal support to the successful Spire Appeal, launched in 1985, raising more than £6.5 million, and culminating in the great televised celebration in AD 2000.

and

The Friends of Salisbury Cathedral – for continuing to contribute, since their formation in 1930, to the beauty of this matchless building – for the greater glory of God.

ACKNOWLEDGEMENTS AND THANKS

In preparing this book I owe thanks to many people, especially to Alun Williams and Michelle Walter of Salisbury Cathedral Visitor Services; to Jane Standen of the Salisbury and South Wiltshire Museum; to Mary Pocock of the Tourist Information Centre, Salisbury; and to Bruce Purvis, Local Studies Librarian, Salisbury (Wiltshire County Council).

The following acknowledgements are also made, with grateful thanks:
Page 20, the paragraph by Alec Clifton-Taylor is taken from *The Cathedrals of England* by Alec Clifton-Taylor, © c.1967 and 1986, Thames & Hudson Ltd, London. Reprinted by kind permission of Thames & Hudson Ltd.
Pages 54–5, the map of Salisbury was provided through the kind permission of the Salisbury Information Centre, and my thanks to Mary Pocock, Tourism Manager, for advice on this.
Page 83, the 'Gruesome hand' photograph was provided by Rupert Willcocks, Landlord of the Haunch of Venison, Minster Street, Salisbury.
Page 89, the photograph of William Golding is © Caroline Forbes.
Page 96, the photograph of the Doom Painting is reproduced by kind permission of David Robson, ABIPP, FSAI, and the Rector of St Thomas's Church.
Pages 104–5, photographs of the Wishford Dancers were provided by the Wishford Oak Apple Club.
Illustrations on pp. 3, 75, 100, 101, & 103 are © Salisbury and South Wiltshire Museum.
Photographs on pp. viii, 7 (the windlass, Steve Day), 14, 17, 36 (the ancient clock, Steve Day), 43, 46 (panel from the Rex Whistler Prism, Peter Marsh), 47 (cadaver effigy of Thomas Bennett, Steve Day), 50 (West Front of the cathedral, Peter Marsh), 57 (detail of Prisoners of Conscience Window, Steve Day), 59, 65 (Hertfort Memorial, Steve Day), are © Salisbury Cathedral.

All other photographs and pen drawings are copyright David Hilliam.

ABOUT THE AUTHOR

David Hilliam grew up in George Herbert's parish of Bemerton on the outskirts of Salisbury, where he went to the village school and sang in the church choir. He was then educated at Bishop Wordsworth's School in Salisbury, being taught by William Golding. Studying and making music in Salisbury Cathedral and its Close, he developed a lifelong passion for the city and its history. After Cambridge and Oxford he taught in Versailles, Kent College Canterbury, and Bournemouth School. Other books by him and also published by Suttons include: *Kings, Queens, Bones and Bastards*; *Monarchs, Murders and Mistresses*; and *Crown, Orb & Sceptre*. He now lives and lectures in Dorset.

INDEX

John Halle was one of Salisbury's wealthiest and most colourful medieval characters, gaining his fortune from the wool trade. He was four times Mayor of Salisbury in the fifteenth century and a part of his impressive house is now the foyer of the Odeon cinema in New Canal (see page 107). He died in 1479.

This drawing, showing John Halle carrying a dagger and wearing striking parti-coloured stockings and preposterous shoes, is taken from a stained-glass window still to be seen in the cinema's entrance hall.